STARS OF TOMORROW

Founded in 1868, B.P.O.E. has grown from a few members in one lodge to nearly a million members in thousands of lodges across the United States.

STARS OF TOMORROW

B.P.O.E. ELKS: PAST, PRESENT & FUTURE

J. Herbert Klein

INTERNATIONAL FA PUBLISHING

LOS ANGELES, CALIFORNIA

STARS OF TOMORROW

ISBN-13: 978-0983028079

ISBN-10: 0983028079

Cover photo: Composite by Mike Everleth

International FA Publishing
3183 Wilshire Blvd., Suite 196 (C38)
Los Angeles, CA 90010
310-607-4957
internationalfilmarts@ymail.com
internationalfapublishing.com

This book is dedicated to members of the

Benevolent Protective Order of the Elks

in appreciation for your

selfless devotion to our country and its citizens,

and for your far-reaching programs

that touch millions of lives each year.

Elks truly do care, and Elks truly do share!

I will donate all my royalties from the sale of this book

to B.P.O.E. and its charities!

The HOME OF HOSPITALITY

Since the mid-1800s, the Elks has been an oasis of friendship, fellowship, and hospitality for its members and their families.

TABLE OF CONTENTS

When I joined the Elks on Flag Day in 1951, I became a member of Los Angeles Lodge #99 at 6th and Parkview, near MacArthur Park. Designed by renowned architect Claude Beelman in the Neo-Gothic style and built in the early 1920s, the building is listed in the National Register of Historic Places and is a designated City of Los Angeles Historic-Cultural monument. After the Elks sold the building, it was turned into a luxury hotel and now stands as a location for films, television programs, and special events. Over thirty movies and TV shows – including *Barton Fink*, *Bugsy*, and *Falcon Crest* – have been filmed at the site, considered one of the most elegant in Los Angeles.

INTRODUCTION

J. Herbert Klein

When I left the army in August 1945, it was a few weeks before my twenty-fourth birthday. My father had died the same day the war ended, but I had little time to grieve. It was up to me to take over the family business – building luxury homes in the Los Angeles area.

My hectic schedule left little time for recreation – I was spending every free minute completing the homes my father had left unfinished when he'd passed away. Still, my Army buddies kept calling and asking to get together, but I had to beg off – until someone suggested we meet at Los Angeles Elks Lodge #99, where he was a member.

Since the lodge was in a convenient location not far from my midtown office, I agreed – and that was the start of my association with the Benevolent Protective Order of the Elks (B.P.O.E.). I became a member of Los Angeles Lodge #99 in 1951 – and I've been stopping by the Elks for social gatherings, dinners, dances, and community fundraisers ever since.

The Elks turned out to be a terrific place to connect with other professionals – at the time, anyone who was anyone belonged to the organization. It was a place to network before anybody thought of the term – the lodge's relaxed setting and inviting atmosphere made it a perfect spot for people to make connections.

I must say that as a professional builder, I was awestruck by the beauty and grandeur of the lodge's building in the MacArthur Park area. It was a testament to the style, class, and vision of the Elks as an organization.

ELKS CLUB 99, LOS ANGELES, CALIFORNIA.

VINTAGE POSTCARDS OF LOS ANGELES LODGE #99

FOYER FROM LOUNGE
ELKS TEMPLE "99" LOS ANGELES

According to numerous news reports, in many areas of the country a new generation is discovering the value of joining the Elks. Today's forty-and-under crowd is finding the Elks a great place to meet after work with friends and colleagues for inexpensive refreshments – and the best part is that most of the proceeds go to charity. The younger set also finds the Elks a terrific place to make friends and business contacts – plus get involved in the community.

Today, I belong to Elks Lodge #906 in Santa Monica, California, where I've been a member now for decades. I wrote this book to express my appreciation for the Elks and to draw new members into the fold. In these pages, I'll explore the Order's history, what's going on today, and what we can do to ensure a bright future for the B.P.O.E.

And, best of all, I'll donate all of my royalties from the sale of this book to B.P.O.E. and its charities.

Chapter One

ELKS EARLY DAYS

Charles Algernon Sidney Vivian arrived in the Port of New York on
November 15, 1867. The crowded, difficult voyage from England
on a large sailing vessel took nearly two months.

THE STORY OF THE BENEVOLENT Protective Order of Elks began on a chilly autumn afternoon in 1868, when twenty-one-year-old Charles Algernon Vivian stepped off an English trading vessel in the Port of New York. Vivian had spent the past two months at sea traveling from Southampton, England, on a vast sailing ship. When he set foot on dry land for the first time, his legs were as unsteady as a baby's, which was fitting – because he was taking his first steps into his new life in America. Like many before him, he had arrived with just the clothes on his back.

For the previous few years, Charles had worked as a comic performer and singer in the music halls of London, where he'd become a crowd favorite and earned glowing reviews. A well-known critic said Charles showed more talent than performers three times his age.

Still, opportunities weren't as plentiful as Charles would have liked. At the time, several old pros – including George Laybourne, Alfred Vance, and Harry Clifton – dominated the London stage, and newcomers had to bide their time waiting for a big break. But Charles was in a hurry to make his mark in the world and had not one minute to spare.

He decided to set his sights on New York – the center of glamour and excitement, where people came from far and wide to see the latest and greatest entertainments.

So now he was in this magical place and ready to prove his worth – all he needed was an opportunity. But he knew no one, had not one friend or acquaintance in the whole big, booming town. He shivered in the cold, realizing he was truly alone in a new land. He buttoned his pea coat, pulled down his knit cap, then stopped one of the men carting luggage and asked where the singers and actors congregated. The man told him to try John Ireland's place, The Star, on Lispenard Street, near Broadway.

Charles asked for directions along the way as he strolled toward his destination, all the while growing steadier on his feet. He was in America, the land of his dreams – and vowed to make good, and help others whenever he could.

The son of a clergyman, Charles and his older brother George had been brought up to live according to the eternal virtues – charity, justice, brotherly love, and fidelity. His parents were no longer on this earth, but he felt they were watching over him and encouraging him to walk the right path.

Step by step, Charles grew more excited and full of joy as he traveled the cobblestone streets of New York. He almost felt like bursting into a song and dance, the kind of entertainments he performed back home in England. He couldn't wait to get started on the New York stage and especially to make the acquaintance of other entertainers.

In England, the entertainers had banded together in social groups and associations that assisted each other in good times and bad. One such organization, the Antediluvian Order of the Buffalo, was a fraternal group that looked out for the welfare of its members. Another was the Dramatic, Musical, and Equestrian Fund, for which he'd heard Mr. Dickens solicit contributions nearly two years before. Charles hoped to find a welcoming fraternal group now that he was in New York.

All around him, people were darting here and there, full of purpose and vitality. The country's Civil War had ended two years before and America was finally becoming a unified nation once again. People seemed happy and excited just to be alive on this crisp November day.

Charles passed rows of buildings where new suits were on display, and he stopped and gazed in each window – noting the style of clothing popular in New York and deciding which suit he'd purchase as soon as he had a few dollars in his pockets.

As it was, he only had one British pound in his pocket, and when he saw a tall white buildings with Greek columns in front, he figured it was a bank – and he'd go inside and exchange his currency for American legal tender.

Inside the grand bank, he felt dwarfed by the vaulted ceilings and hushed atmosphere of wealth. All eyes were on him as he stepped toward a man behind a marble counter outfitted with beveled glass. Charles took off his hat and held it to his chest, then removed his one-pound sterling coin from his jacket pocket and slid it onto the counter.

The elegantly dressed banker pushed up his wire-framed glasses and peered at the single coin presented before him.

"And what can I do for you, young man?" the banker asked.

"Well, sir," Charles responded, "I am newly arrived in your beautiful land and will need native currency with which to conduct my affairs."

"And how would you like your money?" the banker asked.

"Well, how much will it be?" Charles wanted to know.

"That British pound will bring you a bit less than seven dollars in United States currency."

"Give me a stack of every kind of coin you have then," Charles responded, smiling at the thought of how much American money he would soon possess.

The banker sighed and nodded, saying, "As you wish, young man."

As the coins piled up before him, Charles studied their faces. He pulled a shiny copper two-cent piece out of a stack, breathed on it and polished it on his sleeve. He studied the inscription on the coin – In God We Trust – and decided that this shiny new coin would from then on be his good luck piece and symbolic of his new life in America.

When he arrived in America in 1867, Charles Vivian changed his English currency for U.S. money – and, from the coins, picked one that became his lucky two-cent piece, like the one pictured above. The U.S. treasury had recently added the words "In God We Trust" to the coin, inspiring Charles to hold one while praying for guidance.

When the banker had placed all the coins before him, Charles grabbed handfuls and stuffed the coins in the pockets of his jacket. Then he nodded to the banker and said, "Watch for me, for I'm sure I will soon appear on one of your illustrious stages. My name is Charles Vivian."

With that, Charles put on his cap, stuffed his hands in his pockets – enjoying the warm feeling the coins gave him – and made his way toward his destination: the Star on Lispenard Street.

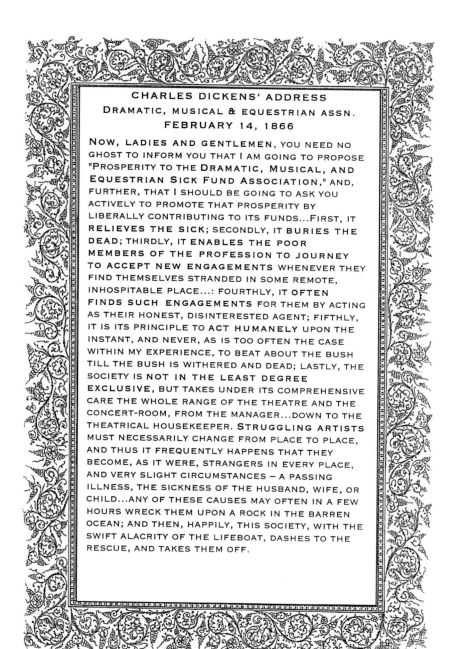

CHARLES DICKENS' ADDRESS
DRAMATIC, MUSICAL & EQUESTRIAN ASSN.
FEBRUARY 14, 1866

NOW, LADIES AND GENTLEMEN, YOU NEED NO GHOST TO INFORM YOU THAT I AM GOING TO PROPOSE "PROSPERITY TO THE DRAMATIC, MUSICAL, AND EQUESTRIAN SICK FUND ASSOCIATION," AND, FURTHER, THAT I SHOULD BE GOING TO ASK YOU ACTIVELY TO PROMOTE THAT PROSPERITY BY LIBERALLY CONTRIBUTING TO ITS FUNDS...FIRST, IT RELIEVES THE SICK; SECONDLY, IT BURIES THE DEAD; THIRDLY, IT ENABLES THE POOR MEMBERS OF THE PROFESSION TO JOURNEY TO ACCEPT NEW ENGAGEMENTS WHENEVER THEY FIND THEMSELVES STRANDED IN SOME REMOTE, INHOSPITABLE PLACE...: FOURTHLY, IT OFTEN FINDS SUCH ENGAGEMENTS FOR THEM BY ACTING AS THEIR HONEST, DISINTERESTED AGENT; FIFTHLY, IT IS ITS PRINCIPLE TO ACT HUMANELY UPON THE INSTANT, AND NEVER, AS IS TOO OFTEN THE CASE WITHIN MY EXPERIENCE, TO BEAT ABOUT THE BUSH TILL THE BUSH IS WITHERED AND DEAD; LASTLY, THE SOCIETY IS NOT IN THE LEAST DEGREE EXCLUSIVE, BUT TAKES UNDER ITS COMPREHENSIVE CARE THE WHOLE RANGE OF THE THEATRE AND THE CONCERT-ROOM, FROM THE MANAGER...DOWN TO THE THEATRICAL HOUSEKEEPER. STRUGGLING ARTISTS MUST NECESSARILY CHANGE FROM PLACE TO PLACE, AND THUS IT FREQUENTLY HAPPENS THAT THEY BECOME, AS IT WERE, STRANGERS IN EVERY PLACE, AND VERY SLIGHT CIRCUMSTANCES — A PASSING ILLNESS, THE SICKNESS OF THE HUSBAND, WIFE, OR CHILD...ANY OF THESE CAUSES MAY OFTEN IN A FEW HOURS WRECK THEM UPON A ROCK IN THE BARREN OCEAN; AND THEN, HAPPILY, THIS SOCIETY, WITH THE SWIFT ALACRITY OF THE LIFEBOAT, DASHES TO THE RESCUE, AND TAKES THEM OFF.

Charles Vivian was present on February 16, 1866 when novelist Charles Dickens gave a speech to raise money for a benevolent association that benefited performers and other theater workers. The great writer's words stayed with Charles as he formulated his ideas for the association that would become the Elks.

As he strolled along, Charles wondered how long he would be able to survive on the coins in his pockets. The most important thing was to find a job straightaway so he could make enough to cover his expenses. He hoped, too, to save money for a rainy day – and, in the entertainment profession, there were always plenty of those.

Charles felt his stomach grumble and figured it was time for his first American meal – he'd heard that the New York taverns offered free lunches with a pint of beer. But it was getting on four o'clock, too late for a mid-day meal. Rather than stop and find a place to grab a bite, Charles decided to keep moving toward his destination. The most important thing today was to find other entertainers and get advice on where to obtain a room and how to get work.

Finally, he was standing in front of The Star Hotel at 60-62 Lispenard Street. He gazed up at the building and smiled. The white bricks seemed to glow in the fading sunshine. It was nearly five in the afternoon and men were crowding into the building for their evening meals.

When Charles stepped into The Star, the aroma of grilled steaks caused his stomach to rumble and the sound of piano music made his spirits lift.

He'd promised himself to practice thrift and watch his pennies, but tonight he needed to celebrate his first day in this city so full of promise. At the door, a blackboard proclaimed in yellow chalk: STEAK & POTATOES 25 CENTS. Charles reached in his jacket pocket and jangled his coins. He was about to spend his first bit of cash.

When Charles Vivian arrived in New York City in 1867, the American Civil War had been over for several years. The country was in the process of getting back on its feet after the four-year war that pitted North against South. People were in festive moods and looking for fun and excitement. The center of entertainment was the Broadway section of New York City, where Charles Vivian hoped to gain employment as a singer and entertainer. These were truly the "old days" – before the arrival of the automobile, telephone, or radio.

Charles entered the restaurant, placed his order at the bar, and then took a seat near the piano player. When the musician turned to a waiter and asked for ale, Charles recognized the man's London accent.

"Brother," Charles said, standing and holding out his hand.

The piano player smiled and said, "From Devonshire, I take it."

Charles felt a bit sheepish that his companion had noted his West County birthplace and he had only spoken one word. He hoped his accent wouldn't be too thick for his American audiences to understand. The good part was that his accent smoothed out considerably when he sang.

After Charles nodded and introduced himself, the piano player said, "I'm Dick Steirly. I play here, there, and everywhere."

"I hope to say the same soon," Charles told him, then shared a bit about his background in London music halls.

Just then, a small man with a big head of hair came between Charles and the musician and said, "Back to business now, Steirly."

"Right so, Mr. Harding," Steirly replied and took his place at the piano.

Harding seemed to stand on his tiptoes as he scanned the crowd, looking from one side of the room to the other.

"As you know, this is Friday," Harding said, addressing the audience. "And today at The Star anyone can share his talents."

Charles couldn't believe his good fortune. He'd happened upon this place on the very night when the management encouraged members of the audience to perform.

"Do we have anyone ready to entertain our patrons?" he asked.

Charles stepped forward just as a waiter was placing his evening meal on the bar. He had to decide whether to satisfy his growling stomach or his hunger for a chance to perform.

He unbuttoned his coat and removed his hat, placing them on a nearby chair. Then he took a deep breath, smoothed his hair with both hands, and stepped forward.

"I would like to volunteer my services," Charles told Harding.

Harding looked Charles up and down and said, "First time?" But it sounded like "foist time." This was Charles's first encounter with a Brooklyn accent.

"In this country," Charles replied.

"And what's yer moniker?" Harding asked. When Charles didn't respond, Harding explained his meaning by saying: "What's your name?"

Charles realized that if he gave his real name and delivered a substandard performance, he might ruin his chances to get ahead. He decided to give his mother's maiden name.

"Richardson," he told Harding.

"All right, Mr. Richardson," the diminutive Harding said. "Let's hear what you've got."

Like most singers of the day, Charles relied on an original repertoire – songs he'd written and performed since starting on the London stage three years before at age eighteen. Back in England, singers were barred from performing songs from other people's acts. But in America, Charles was free to sing his own songs and any others he'd learned in England.

He decided to start with a bang – his most popular song, "Jimmy Riddle Who Played Upon the Fiddle." Like most of his repertoire, the song was comic in nature and combined singing with recitation. Of course, he couldn't expect the pianist to accompany him right away, but figured Steirly would be able to jump in after the first verse.

Charles stood before the growing crowd, and realized he would be lucky if he could garner even a portion of their attention. Most of the men were busy eating, downing mugs of ale, and gabbing with their friends. He took a deep breath and reached in is vest pocket and felt his lucky two-cent piece. "In God I Trust," he told himself before opening his mouth and praying that his voice would not fail him.

As he sang in his light baritone the tale of the poor young man who falls in love with the girl who runs off with Jimmy Riddle, a chap who plays the fiddle, Charles could hear the place get quieter and quieter until his voice was the only sound in the room.

Steirly began playing before the end of the first stanza – his piano work first-rate. Charles was sure that running into such a consummate musician on his first night in New York was an omen of good things to come.

Charles could feel the audience's total attention as he delivered the final chorus: "His name was Jimmy Riddle and he played upon the fiddle, and he managed for to swindle me of my true love."

People burst into applause, clapping and stomping their feet, sending sawdust flying into the air.

"More! More! More" voices called out.

Charles noticed a tall, slender, silver-haired man call to one of the waiters and say: "Run around the corner and get Bob Butler."

When Charles asked Steirly the identity of the silver-haired man, Steirly replied, "That's the owner, John Ireland."

Just then, master of ceremonies Harding rushed up and told Charles, "Quick. Another song. We need to keep 'em happy."

Charles launched into his next biggest hit, "Who Stole the Donkey," a comic tale about a group of boys making fun of a man's new hat. The crowd greeted this one with even louder applause and cried out for another.

By the time Charles had finished his third song, the waiter had returned with a small, stout man wearing a derby hat. The man approached Charles while the audience clapped and called for another song.

"Johnny sent for me," the man said. "He tells me you're the greatest singer he's ever heard."

Just then John Ireland stepped up, his silver hair shining in the lamplight. Ireland revealed to Charles that he was talking to none other than Robert Butler, manager of the American Theatre on Broadway.

"Go on, now, Richardson" Ireland said. "Show him what you've got."

After Ireland and Butler sat down, Charles resumed his place next to the piano. He took some deep breaths to calm himself, but couldn't shake the feeling that his whole future depended on this one song. Again, he held his lucky two-cent piece in his hand and said to himself, "In God I trust."

When he was finished with the song, he looked over at Butler, who sat there shaking his head. Charles felt he had sung his best, and didn't know how to interpret Butler's reaction. Just then, Butler jumped up and said, "You're the best singer I've heard all year – and it's nearly Thanksgiving."

"Thank you, sir," Charles said, saluting Steirly in appreciation for his expert playing. "Anyone could sing well with an accompanist such as Dick Steirly."

"I'm booking you for three weeks, Richardson," Butler said. "Starting on Monday. Tell me your first name. I'll need it for the posters."

"First name, Charles," Charles said. "Last name, Vivian." Then he explained why he'd given his mother's maiden name at the outset.

"Fifty dollars a week to start," Butler said. "Payable at the end of the week."

With that, Butler turned and strode out of the place and Charles was left with four words ringing in his ears – FIFTY DOLLARS A WEEK! It was more than he'd ever dreamed he'd make in a month.

The rest of the evening seemed like a dream. The crowd encouraged Charles to keep singing and before he knew it, closing time had rolled around. When most of the patrons had left, Mr. Harding came up and pressed two coins into Charles's hand. When Charles looked down, two shining one-dollar silver coins were staring up at him. He thought he'd been singing for free and had had no expectation of payment.

"Fine work," Harding said, then shook Charles's hand. "Hope to see you again soon."

"Thank you, sir," Charles replied, realizing that his lucky two-cent piece had already multiplied itself a hundredfold.

After Harding had made his way to the till to count the evening's take, Steirly asked where Charles was staying.

"I was just about to give that some thought," Charles replied.

Steirly told Charles he knew just the place – his boarding house, which catered to actors and other theater people. He explained that their trade's irregular hours upset most households, but Mrs. Geisman charged extra for the trouble and carved out a nice living for herself.

When Charles inquired about the costs, Steirly told him not to worry – he'd pay his new friend's first week's room and board.

R. R. STEIRLY

"After all, Charles," Steirly said, "you'll soon be rich with the handsome sums Butler is paying you. I've never, ever, seen him offer that much to a newcomer."

"I feel very, very lucky," Charles responded.

"I'll talk with Mrs. Geisman early in the morning. Why don't you come around then," Steirly told Charles, writing the address – 188 Elm Street – on a piece of paper. "For tonight, I'm sure Mr. Ireland will put you up at The Star."

The next day, after he got settled into his lodgings at Mrs. Geisman's boarding house, Charles began to think about his engagement at the American Theatre. He had come to this country with nothing more than the clothes he was wearing. He'd abandoned his seafaring clothes on the ship and had changed into his finest suit just before arriving in the harbor. While the outfit was his best, it wasn't really good enough for a New York opening.

Before he'd left England, Charles had sold everything he owned, clothes included, to buy his passage to America. Until Butler paid him the following week, he didn't have enough money to buy a new suit of clothes – though that's just what he'd wanted to do when he'd passed the clothing shops the previous day.

At lunchtime, he shared a meal with other inhabitants of the boarding house. He was pleased to make the acquaintance of these actors and entertainers – it was just what he'd hoped for upon his arrival in New York.

When Dick Steirly informed the others about Charles's three-week engagement at the American Theatre, his fellow boarders jumped up and clapped him on the back and began to sing, "For He's a Jolly Good Fellow."

After they were finished singing and congratulating him, the men asked if there was anything they could do to help him get ready for his big day.

W. L. BOWRON

Charles pondered whether or not to broach the subject that was heavy on his mind. He didn't want these fellows to look upon him as a pauper; but, on the other hand, they were congenial gents and seemed as if they really wanted to help. Charles cleared his throat and spoke up.

"I would appreciate the loan of a suit of clothes."

The men responded with assents, speaking over one another and sizing up each other to decide who was closest in height and weight to Charles. The likely candidate turned out to be W.L. Bowron, a man of about forty with a wide smile peeking out from under his bushy mustache.

"Happy to help, Charles Vivian," said Bowron. "I can see your name on the marquee now."

The men then whisked Charles to a barbershop and treated him to a haircut and a shave – and his two months at sea were finally a memory, except for a well-trimmed mustache. Charles felt he needed the facial appendage to make himself appear more mature.

"Sometimes," he explained, "people think I'm too young to sing about love, courtship, and the problems of the working man."

When he stepped outside of the barbershop, W.L. Bowron was waiting was his freshly pressed suit on a hanger. He took one look at the beardless Charles Vivian and clapped himself on the forehead.

"Now I recognize you," Bowron said. "I believe we were on the same bill at Major's Hall in London about two years back."

All of those present had a good laugh over that.

That afternoon, many of the men made their way to theaters to perform in matinees, then popped back for a quick dinner before heading out for evening performances. Steirly played piano at one place in the afternoon and two others in the evening, and Charles tagged along to learn what he could before his opening performance.

Charles was struck by Steirly's virtuosity. The man could play anything in any key and easily shift from song to song and mood to mood. As he watched the performances, Charles thought about the kindness and generosity of the men at his boarding house. It was wonderful that the group had formed such a strong bond for his benefit. He hoped he could repay the favor sometime soon.

He thought about his membership in the Antediluvian Order of the Buffalo, the fraternal group that had offered him such friendship and fraternity in England. In a way, these new friends in New York were offering the same kinds of help in an informal way.

During the 1860s, the theater district extended to the lower east side of New York. Called the Bowery, the area was home to many theatrical establishments and music halls.

The following day was Sunday, and Charles felt eager to go for a stroll and take in the sights and sounds of his new home. After a brisk walk to midtown and back, he decided to stop for a pint of ale, but was surprised to learn than all the taverns in New York were closed on Sunday. He wondered if social clubs existed that served more than root beer, and made a note to ask his fellow boarders.

His Monday opening finally arrived, and the audience went wild for his act. The next day, Charles ran out early in the morning for a newspaper, because he'd learned that the press had been at his performance the night before. After plunking down some coins for the paper, Charles rushed through the pages searching for the review. When he finally found it, the words seemed to beam out at him from the newsprint. The best remark was the last sentence, *"He has made a very favorable impression, and will become a favorite at this establishment."*

He was on his way to a career on the American stage! The shows went so well that Butler booked him for nine weeks – all the way through January 25, 1868.

But the first week was the most fulfilling and the most festive for Charles – and his friends at the rooming house. On Sunday, he hosted a party in Mrs. Geisman's large attic – a wonderful spot, equipped with easy chairs and a piano. For the festivities, Charles had purchased the day before a keg of beer – and his fellow revelers cheered him for his foresight.

For the next several weeks, the group met frequently in the attic, which had become their social club – with an initiation fee of fifty cents per person. Soon, more and more men joined the group and the attendees began to overflow the accommodations. The landlady, Mrs. Geisman, put an end to it all – telling the men that they'd have to move their revelry elsewhere because other tenants had complained about the noise.

OPENING NIGHT SENSATION!

After his premiere performance at Butler's American Theatre, 472 Broadway (pictured at right) on November 18, 1867, Charles Vivian received a favorable newspaper review, which read: *"Charles Vivian, a comic singer from the principal music halls of London, England, made his American debut at Butler's American Theatre on the 18th. He possesses one very necessary attribute of a comic singer – that is, he speaks with singular distinctness, and makes himself heard in the most remote parts of the hall. He is practical and, knowing precisely what his audiences require, he gives it to them to their hearts' content. He not only knows how to sing a song, but seems determined to rely upon songs the words of which shall convey some kind of sense, and the music shall possess some distinctive character. He sang an original comic song called 'Who Stole the Donkey,' which was received with thunders of applause, and he was encored four times. Later in the evening, he sang 'Jimmy Riddle What Plays Upon a Fiddle' This is a very laughable song, and pleased the audience so much that he was called out and had to sing four other songs, all of which took well. He has made a very favorable impression, and will be a favorite of the establishment."*

The group soon found a new meeting place at 17 Delancey Street, above Paul Sommer's saloon, and raised the membership fee to two dollars. More and more people began to attend the club, now known as the Jolly Corks for a trick Charles had introduced one evening at Sandy Spencer's Saloon on Broadway. Charles had placed a cork in front of each man at the bar and said the last one to pick it up had to buy drinks all around. Those in the know had figured out not to lift the cork at all, so that when the newcomer lifted his cork, he was the last to pick it up – because he was the only one to do so. Charles was the self-styled Imperial Cork of the club.

The "cork trick" originated at a London tavern, where Charles Vivian learned it the hard way – by losing the game and having to buy drinks for everyone in the place. Soon after arriving in America during 1867, he introduced the custom to his New York friends. Once initiated into the Jolly Corks, a member promised to always carry a cork and produce it whenever requested by a fellow member – or endure the penalty of buying the challenger a drink.

Chapter Two

ELKS BEGINNINGS

The Benevolent and Protective Order of Elks was formally established in New York City on February 16, 1868.

BY THE END OF 1867, CHARLES VIVIAN HAD MADE MANY NEW friends and performed at many locations around New York. At one of these concert halls, Charles met a singer named Ted Quinn – a friendly gentleman who lived to perform on stage. The day after Christmas, Charles learned that Quinn had died the previous day, leaving a young wife and three small children.

Charles and four of his friends from the Jolly Corks attended the funeral, and they were all moved by the grief and distress of Quinn's wife, who huddled with her children, saying, "What will we do? What will we do?"

Back at their headquarters on Delancey Street, the men discussed how they could help Mrs. Quinn and her children. George McDonald stopped by after his evening performance and the others filled him in on what had happened at the funeral. McDonald suggested that they turn the Jolly Corks into a benevolent and protective society – a fraternal organization that looked out for the welfare of its members. This way, they could help the Quinn family and others as the need arose.

They presented the idea to the fifteen core members of the group and all concurred. The group's original members included: Charles Vivian, actor and singer; Richard Steirly, pianist; William Carleton, variety entertainer, songwriter, and playwright; Henry Vandermark, singer; William Lloyd Bowron, theater musician; John T. Kent, Thomas G. Riggs, and George F. McDonald, actors; J.G. Wilson, singer and dancer; John H. Blume, operator of stage lights; Frank Langhorne and M.G. Ashe, theatrical photographers; E.M. Platt, show business employee; and Henry L. Bosworth, costumer.

Vivian appointed a committee to develop a new name for the group – encouraging the men to devise something lofty, grand, and inspiring. "It should be a name for the ages," Charles advised, "a name that fills us with pride."

When Charles Vivian appointed a committee to suggest a name for their fraternal group, the men visited P.T. Barnum's American Museum for inspiration. Mixing elements of a zoo, school, theater, and freak show, the museum featured strange, wonderful, amazing, and exotic displays from around the world – for a twenty-five cent entry fee.

The others knew that Charles considered "buffalo" a proud name, and figured they would narrow their choices to an animal – a distinctly American animal.

The committee members decided to pay a visit to P.T. Barnum's New American Museum, a nearby repository for curiosities from around the world – including an impressive array of both stuffed and live animals. After touring floor after floor filled with displays nearly impossible to believe – the world's tallest and smallest people, a dog that ran a spinning wheel, mummies, whales in glass tanks – they focused on the animals. Barnum's museum had on display more animals than any of the men had ever heard of – and they were stunned at some of the beasts that met their eyes, especially those from Australia. While they didn't want to be known as the Order of the Platypus, they were partial to two animals they'd viewed at the museum: the moose and the elk – real American wildlife.

They agreed to present these choices to their fellow members when they convened in February.

Meanwhile, there was another move in the offing – the group had to vacate 17 Delancey after just four weeks. While members looked for a suitable meeting place, the men got to know just about every piece of real estate in Manhattan. But their choices were limited because they had to keep expenses low – after all, there were just fifteen dues-paying members. Then again, they had to find a big enough space to accommodate an influx of new members. The trick was to find a large space with small rent.

One Sunday, nine of the men were traveling together, looking at spaces to lease. At one building at the corner of Chambers and Chatham, they chanced upon the photography studio of K.W. Beniczky and decided while they were together to have their formal photograph taken by a professional.

Photography was still a novelty, and when the men entered the studio they were in awe of the ornate set pieces used for backgrounds as well as the complex photographic equipment. The men weren't alone in wanting to sit for a photograph on their day off. People were lined up for a chance to capture their images for all time. As luck would have it, one of the group's members, F. C. Langhorn, was working at the studio and managed to get his colleagues to the head of the line. He separated the group into two and joined his fellows in the photo taken by a photographer named M.G. Ash. Langhorn then snapped a photograph of the other five members. Later, Langhorn mounted the two photos together so it looked as if all the men had been photographed at once.

ORIGINATORS of the B.P.O.ELKS-1868.

Ten of the fifteen founding members of the Benevolent and Protective Order of Elks are pictured in the above photo, taken at K.W. Beniczky's photo studio in January 1868. Charles Vivian is in the front row, third from the right.

After their photo session, the men managed to find a perfect location for their growing group. They couldn't wait to tell the group about the new building – and try to arrange for all members to gather for a group photo. But the entertainers' busy schedules made it impossible for everyone to get together at the same time.

On February 16, 1868, the naming committee reported at the group's new meeting place on the upper floor of Military Hall, located at 193 Bowery. Members of the naming committee recommended that their group call itself the Benevolent and Protective Order of Elks. Charles Vivian told those present that he preferred Order of Buffalo, and put the matter to a vote. Of the fifteen members, seven voted for the name buffalo, but elk carried the day with eight votes.

W.L. Bowron, the man who'd loaned Charles a suit for his initial American engagement, at first intended to vote "buffalo," but changed his mind at the last moment and cast his vote for "elk."

When the matter was settled, Thomas Riggs jumped up and shouted, "I'm glad to be an Elk, as I was born on Elk Street in the City of Buffalo."

All the men rallied around the new name and began to call each other "Brother Elk." Their first order of business was to take up a collection for Quinn's family.

The following month, The Benevolent Protective Order of Elks adopted its constitution, which stated that the Order was organized to "promote, protect, and enhance the welfare and happiness of each other." This mission centered on the cardinal principles of fidelity, brotherly love, justice, and charity. The rules included meeting once a week and setting initiation fees at two dollars and weekly dues at twenty-five cents.

To learn more about their namesake, a group of Elks turned to a nearby institution – the Cooper Union. Dedicated to art and science, the school offered the men opportunities to speak with instructors in the natural sciences and visit the school's impressive library. At the location, they examined a natural history book that described the elk as an animal that was fast ("fleet of foot"), noble ("timorous of doing wrong") and brave ("ever ready to combat in defense of self or of the female of the species").

This description appealed to the committee because the elk's characteristics – swiftness, courage, and nobility – fit their vision for the fraternal group they were founding.

Established in 1859 by Peter Cooper, a self-educated business tycoon, the Cooper Union for the Advancement of Science and Art was founded to provide educational opportunities for qualified people with limited resources. Members of the newly christened Benevolent Protective Order of Elks visited Cooper Union to discuss the attributes of the elk with natural scientists and review the school's collection of books on natural history.

B.P.O.E. original charter, 1868

The Elks continued to grow at an amazing rate, and within twenty years established one hundred lodges with over ten thousand members.

A few years after arriving in America, Charles Vivian turned his sights west and headed for California, performing in San Francisco, where he met his future wife, a singer named Imogen Holbrook. Together, they traveled throughout the Western states giving musical and dramatic performances.

Their travels eventually led them to Leadville, Colorado, then a booming mining town, and the second largest city in the state. Charles and his wife experienced a variety of hardships while performing in the town, and Charles's health suffered due to Leadville's extremely high altitude of nearly eleven thousand feet. The mountainous region was frigid, and the Vivians were unable to secure accommodations with adequate heat. Charles was stricken with what doctors diagnosed as pneumonia and after a weeklong battle with fever and delirium, he passed away in the early morning hours of Saturday, March 20, 1880.

The locals organized a benefit to pay for Charles's funeral, held at the Tabor Opera House. The entire town turned out to pay tribune to Charles and thousands had to be turned away from the services. All the mourners took part in a procession to the gravesite, while musicians played Charles' repertoire of songs, including his favorite, "Ten Thousand Miles Away."

A professional performer since his teenage years, Charles Vivian gave his final performances in Leadville, Colorado, during the late winter of 1860. He directed and starred in a production of *Oliver Twist* at the Leadville Amphitheater, and sang at the Theatre Comique (pictured above in left of photo) and the Woods Theatre. With the mountains in the background and the unpaved, frontier streets, this photo gives a sense of Charles Vivian's dedication to his art – visiting remote, rustic places to perform for people eager to connect with the outside world.

CHARLES VIVIAN, founder of B.P.O.E.

(1846-1880)

A BIOGRAPHICAL SKETCH
OF
Charles A. S. Vivian
FOUNDER OF
THE ORDER OF ELKS

IMOGEN HOLBROOK VIVIAN

After her husband's passing, Imogen Vivian wrote a book-length remembrance of Charles Vivian, published in 1904, more than twenty years after his death. During their marriage, the Vivians traveled throughout the West giving recitations, concerts, and theatrical performances. When they staged *Oliver Twist*, based on the Dickens novel, Charles played the Artful Dodger and Imogen played Oliver Twist.

Vivian's widow made sure her husband would be remembered as the founder of the Elks by writing a biography, published in 1904. In her book, she recounts her adventures touring the Western United States with her husband as a performer. She believed he worked himself to exhaustion trying to bring joy to others through his talents.

Toward the end of her book, she writes: *"The greater part of Charles Vivian's life was spent in his endeavors to make others happy, and those who remember him best can testify as to how well he succeeded in enabling them for a time, at least, to forget the trials and cares of everyday life, while listening to this prince of entertainers. That he sacrificed himself professionally and financially upon the altar of the club and social circle, there is not the shadow of a doubt. In being able to give others pleasure, he best pleased himself...he was always a leader in club circles, never a follower, owing to his wonderful gift of entertaining; his recognized superiority in such matters; his strong personal magnetism, and the preference of his fellows."*

Charles Vivian became ill shortly after arriving in Leadville, Colorado, and passed away from pneumonia at age thirty-four. The town held a benefit for his funeral expenses and his services were held at the Tabor Opera House (pictured above) – a fitting tribute for a man who'd lived nearly half of his life on stage.

The local newspaper, *The Leadville Chronicle*, wrote of him, "Charles Vivian was a man of many friends, whom his kindly nature and genial manners drew toward him, and many a tear has been today in the eyes of strong men, who will miss his cheery voice. Brilliant, witty, educated, intelligent, and convivial, his very presence enthused the dullest company from the first moment of his appearance, with a life and spirit unimaginable to those unacquainted with him. He has no successor in either stage or social circles."

In America, Charles Vivian achieved many of his dreams – a career on the stage, a happy marriage, and founding a thriving fraternal order. In thirty-four short years, he'd lived a full life.

In 1889, nine years after his death, Elks Lodge #10 in Boston, Massachusetts, raised funds for a monument to Charles Vivian and paid for his body's transport to its new home at Mt. Hope Cemetery in Boston.

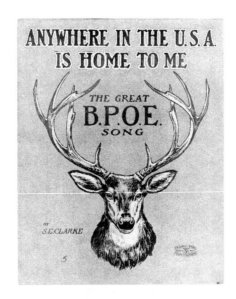

Over the decades, many writers have been inspired to write songs dedicated to the Elks.

Today, few of the buildings that hosted the beginnings of Elkdom are still standing. But one important landmark remains – a two-block stretch of Elm Street, where Charles Vivian boarded at Mrs. Geisman's, has been designated Elk Street to commemorate the early years of the Benevolent Protective Order of Elks.

In 1939, New York Mayor Fiorello LaGuardia – a member of the Elks – approved a proposal to change two blocks of Elm Street to Elk Street.

Chapter Three
ELKS PRINCIPLES

The Elks' stated purpose is to "foster the happiness and well-being of its members and to live the principles of charity, justice, brotherly love, and fidelity."

SINCE ITS FORMAL FOUNDING ON FEBRUARY 16, 1868, THE Order of Elks has worked diligently to live out its principles of charity, justice, brotherly love, and fidelity. For generations, the order has raised hundreds of millions of dollars for a host of worthy causes, living out the motto, "Elks Care, Elks Share."

Elks act quickly in times of need, responding with, in the words of Fred Harper, Grand Exalted Ruler (1917-1918): *"Food to the hungry; shelter for the homeless; clothes and fuel for the needy; milk for undernourished babies; medical attention to the sick; baskets to the poor at Christmas and Thanksgiving; outings for underprivileged children; entertainment to shut-ins; work for the unemployed; artificial limbs for the maimed; hospital beds; free clinics; night schools and...care for and entertainment of the members of the Armed Forces. And the list might be indefinitely extended."*

In his address, Grand Exalted Ruler Harper also mentioned Elks State Associations, which work in their local areas and communities to address specific needs and member concerns. Lodges make provisions for scholarships, medical care, veterans' needs, and other worthy causes within their spheres. Grand exalted Ruler Harper reflected: *"No history of social service in the United States would be complete without an inspiring chapter devoted to the achievements of the Order of the Elks in this field."*

It is good to be reminded of the cardinal principles that guide the Elks and to reflect on their meaning. For this, let's turn to the writings of Grand Exalted Ruler Meade D. Detweiler, who served multiple terms as Grand Exalted Ruler in the late 1890s. An attorney by profession, Detweiler was an eloquent speaker and gifted writer. His profound commitment to the B.P.O.E. is most often remembered in his tireless work to make the Elks National Home a reality. Throughout his lifetime, Grand Exalted Ruler Detweiler spent much time reflecting on the Elks and the Order's higher purposes.

Meade D. Detweiler (1863-1904), joined Elks Lodge #12, Harrisburg, Pennsylvania, in 1892, and was elected Grand Exalted Ruler in 1895, 1896, and 1897. An attorney, Detweiler was active in Pennsylvania politics, running for the state senate. He often spoke about the Elks and authored many writings about the Order, including a full-length book entitled *An Account of the Origin and Early History of the Benevolent and Protective Order of the Elks of the U.S.A* (1898). As shown in the drawing above, he wore his Elks pin with pride.

CHARITY: "Let ours be the broad charity of love and help to all God's creatures – the charity that will lift up the lowly and champion the cause of the downtrodden and oppressed, a charity bounded by no narrow lines of prejudice, no hereditary transmission of bigotry, from ignorance begotten of old-time feuds. Let ours be the charity that thinketh no ill, that believeth not the tale that compasses a brother's hurt – a charity possessed of a patient endurance that is godlike – a charity that, recognizing the brotherhood of man and the fatherhood of God, aims to raise all mankind to higher and nobler models and loftier aspirations – a charity that throws the mantle of forgiveness and oblivious over the foibles of others – that, realizing that man is his brother's keeper, seeks to make every act of life a benediction of joy to some voyager of life's ocean, which shall undulate the ever widening wavelets of influence upon the shores of eternity."

JUSTICE: "The fundamental principles of security and integrity in society – that, without which all good things in thought or action, all progressive developments, all achievement of art and science or morality and belles lettres of statesmanship and social consolidation would disappear in the wild convulsions of an elemental chaos. By justice, nations are preserved, and by justice kingdoms or individuals alike eventually fall beneath the iron heel of retribution. Justice never fails."

BROTHERLY LOVE: "There are no diviner words of apostle, evangelist, or seer than the simple utterance, 'Let brotherly love continue.' And yet simple as it is, sublimity breathes from every word and irradiates each letter. The schools of philosophy, from Socrates to Emerson, have never produced a more sententious expression to inculcate the great fundamental doctrines underlying the laws of life and being. With brotherly love, this world would become an Eden and generous garlands of perfumed flowers crown every milestone on the weary march of life. Without it, earth becomes a Sahara of woe, marked at every step amid the shifting sands with phantom forms and ghastly, grinning skeletons of dead hopes and blighted affections."

FIDELITY: "Only he who is faithful to death shall wear the crown. It is not enough for a time to exercise a charity boundless as the great ocean. It is not enough, for a time, to hold the scales with a poise to equal that the different sides vary but by a hair's breadth. It is not enough, for a time, to write each foible in the sand in front of the tide rapidly advancing to its obliteration whilst every virtue has been deeply graven on columns of adamant. It is necessary that charity and justice and brotherly love continue to their full tide of glory – that the devotion to duty end only with life."

Let's look at some highlights over the decades of how Elks have demonstrated the cardinal principles.

In February 1904, Notre Dame professor and coach Frank E. Hering, a member of Elks Lodge #235 in South Bend, Indiana, is the first to propose a national Mother's Day.

When a devastating earthquake strikes San Francisco in 1906, the Elks respond quickly. Remarking on the order's efforts, Robert W. Brown, Grand Exalted Ruler at the time, says: _"A blessed distinction of the Elk is that he has practiced in the heavenly art of charity...and the Elk was quick to respond. He knew precisely what to do and how to do it."_ Before the government steps in to help, the Elks have already set up a tent city for the homeless.

In 1936, B.P.O.E. donates approximately $130,000 to victims of the Pittsburgh floods.

Past Grand Exalted Ruler Raymond Benjamin, vice chairman of the Elks National Foundation, left, and Past Grand Exalted Ruler John F. Malley, right, congratulate Jean Ann Lawson and Gilbert R. Panzer on their scholarship awards in this 1950 photo taken at the Grand Lodge Session in Miami.

During the early 1950s, the U.S. Government asks the B.P.O.E. to solicit blood donations from its membership – and members respond with 600,000 pints for soldiers serving in Korea.

President Harry Truman (left) congratulates high school student William Johnson on winning first prize – a $1,000 bond – for his essay "Why Democracy Works." Joining in the celebration is George I. Hall (right) Grand Exalted Ruler of the Elks, sponsor of the contest, which awards over one hundred thousand dollars in prizes.

in 1972, the Elks introduces Hoop Shoot, a youth program, nationwide. In 1976, Grand Exalted Ruler George B. Klein dedicates an Elks Hoop Shoot Plaque at the Basketball Hall Of Fame.

In 1951, Grand Exalted Ruler Joseph B. Kyle (seated, right) presents President Truman (seated, left) with the Elks' pledge of its membership for civil defense activities.

Chapter Four

AMERICAN PRESIDENTS

**Five U.S. presidents – Democrats and Republicans alike –
have belonged to the Benevolent Protective Order of Elks.**

ELECTED OFFICIALS ARE CHARGED WITH UPHOLDING THE public good. Many politicians get in touch with their constituents by getting involved in civic, community, and fraternal organizations. The Elks is a great proving ground for many of these leaders. They learn about the values and concerns of private citizens, what moves people, what makes them tick (and tock!), and how to gain support in a community.

The Benevolent Protective Order of Elks attracts the best and the brightest – and its membership has included five United States presidents. In this chapter, we'll review the biographies of these individuals, learn why they joined the Elks, and examine why the organization was an important part of their identities.

These individuals have left a legacy of leadership, vision, public service, and dedication to their fellow man. Let's take a look at their lives – and their lodges.

Warren G. Harding (1865-1923), the 29th president of the
United States, served as executive in chief from 1921-1923,
the years following the end of World War I. In the above
photo, he is relaxing at the Elks National Home in Bedford,
Virginia, after speaking at the dedication ceremonies. In 1890,
he joined Elks Lodge #32 in Marion, Ohio.

Before entering politics, Warren G. Harding published a newspaper in Marion, Ohio, a town of about thirty-five thousand people. He joined the Elks in 1890, when he was twenty-five years old, and a few years later served as Esteemed Loyal Knight.

A reserved man, Harding was surprised when fellow Elks showed up at his newspaper office and explained they were on the Memorial Day Committee and wanted him to deliver the memorial address. He tried to convince the committee members to find someone else, but his wife persuaded him to "help the boys out."

Members of the lodge responded to Harding's speech with enthusiasm and applause – success that led the young newspaperman to take up public speaking. In 1899, he entered politics – running for and winning a seat in the Ohio State Senate. Harding was elected Lieutenant Governor of Ohio in 1904, U.S. senator in 1915, and U.S. president in 1920, when he defeated the Democratic ticket, which included Franklin D. Roosevelt as vice president.

In 1922, President Harding spoke at a special banquet at the Marion, Ohio, Elks Lodge to commemorate the city's centennial. Celebrating the event with President Harding were General John Pershing, Grand Exalted Ruler William Mountain, the governor and attorney general of Ohio, and the president of the Ohio Elks Association.

Harding died at the age of 57 while serving his first term in office. His legacy includes signing the peace treaty with Germany and Austria that formally ended World War I, signing into law the first children's social services program, and heading an administration where unemployment was cut in half.

Political historian Carl S. Anthony summed up Harding's presidential career by calling him, "A modern figure who embraced technology and culture; sensitive to the plights of minorities, women, and labor."

LODGE #32, MARION, OHIO

Marion, Ohio, Elks Lodge #32 marked its beginning on March 3, 1885, less than twenty years after the founding of the Order. Up to this point in Elks history, lodges had only been established in big cities. The Marion, Ohio, Lodge bears the distinction as the first small community Elks lodge in the United States.

The second Elks lodge established in Ohio, the Marion lodge opened with thirty-three charter members. After renting space around town for nearly thirty years, the lodge finally established a permanent home in 1914, when the membership moved into the town's Grand Opera House, which the lodge had purchased the year before. Thirty years later, in 1945, the building was paid off. The lodge is still situated in this location.

As with most Elks lodges, this one experienced some ups and downs and increases and decreases in membership. The Depression years during the 1930s represented an especially difficult time; membership fell off dramatically as people struggled to stay alive. Elks member William Guitery made a donation during this period for funds to purchase a burial plot in Marion Cemetery so every Marion Elk would be assured a final resting place. The Marion Lodge is one of only a few Elks Lodges to offer a benefit of this type.

The lodge is especially proud of its most illustrious member – Warren G. Harding, who joined in 1890 as the lodge's sixty-eighth member. Harding remained involved in Elks activities even after his election as president.

Members of the Marion Elks provided support and encouragement when a woman from Marion won the Miss Ohio contest and went on to compete in the Miss America contest in Atlantic City, New Jersey, where she was crowned the winner in 1938.

Marion Lodge #32 boasts a U.S. president and a Miss America. It's truly an all-American lodge, with plenty to feel proud about.

Franklin Delano Roosevelt (1882-1945) was the 32nd president of
the United States, serving from 1933 until he died in office in 1945
at age sixty-three. The only president elected to more than two
terms, he is best remembered for inspiring the nation during the
darkest days of the Great Depression in the 1930s. He belonged
to Elks Lodge #275 in Poughkeepsie, New York.

An attorney by profession, Franklin D. Roosevelt entered politics in 1910, when he won a seat in the New York state senate. He served one term as governor of New York before running for president of the United States in 1932. He was elected to four terms.

Roosevelt assumed the presidency during some of America's most challenging days. When he took office, the country had been struggling for three years to regain its footing after the economic collapse ushered in by the stock market crash of October 29, 1929.

Roosevelt's administration developed a variety of initiatives to foster America's economic recovery. Called the New Deal, the programs were aimed at helping Americans get on their feet and get the country back to work. He is widely heralded with serving as a beacon of optimism during very dark days.

Roosevelt was a decisive leader and charismatic public speaker. He reassured the nation that the country would prevail after he signed a declaration of war on Japan following that country's surprise attack on the United States Naval Base in Pearl Harbor, Hawaii, on December 7, 1941. He is remembered for reminding the nation "the only thing we have to fear is fear itself."

In rankings by historians, Roosevelt is consistently listed as the second greatest U.S. president, following Abraham Lincoln. He is also rated as one of the most admired people of the twentieth century.

Roosevelt's legacy includes establishing the March of Dimes to combat polio, an illness he had contracted in his thirties and which left him paralyzed from the waist down for about half of his life. For his work in this area, his image is commemorated on the U.S. dime coin.

The Poughkeepsie, New York, Elks lodge received its charter on June 20, 1894, when Franklin Roosevelt was twelve years old. Roosevelt's father, James, was active in the Order and Franklin became involved at an early age.

Lodge #275 is proud of its illustrious member, Franklin D. Roosevelt and proclaims "home lodge of FDR" on the masthead of its newsletter.

Poughkeepsie, New York, Lodge #275 features a Franklin Delano Roosevelt wall of photos, information, and memorabilia.

President Franklin D. Roosevelt reviews a poster design for the War Department. Elks Grand Exalted Ruler Joseph G. Buch (center) presents the poster, accompanied by (left to right): Past Grand Exalted Ruler James T. Halliman, United States Senator Roger F. Wagner, Chairman James R. Nicholson of the National Defense Commission, and Major Charles S. Hart, who was later elected grand exalted ruler..

Harry S. Truman (1884-1972) was the 33rd president of the United States, succeeding Franklin Delano Roosevelt upon his death in 1945 and serving until 1953. He was commander in chief during the final months of WWII as well as throughout the Korean War. Truman was a member of Elks Lodge #26 in Kansas City, Missouri.

When he became president in April 1945, Harry S. Truman told the press, "Pray for me." He was an ordinary, down-to-earth man thrust into the most important job in the world through a series of extraordinary circumstances. Faced with many difficult decisions, including his directive to use atomic weapons to end the war with Japan, Truman believed "the buck stops here" – meaning, he would make the tough decisions and face the consequences.

Truman came from a humble background, and is the only president in the 20th century who did not attend college – poor eyesight prevented him from pursuing his dream of attending West Point. He wanted to serve the country, and gained entry into the Missouri National Guard by memorizing the eye chart. His artillery unit served in France during WWI, where Truman was elevated to the rank of Captain and credited with great feats of heroism and saving many lives.

After the war, Truman ran a small business in Kansas City and served as an administrator in county government. He entered politics in 1934 – the same year he joined Elks Lodge #26 – when he ran for U.S. senator from Missouri, winning the election. He was reelected in 1942, and in 1944 tapped as Franklin Roosevelt's running mate for his fourth term in office.

A few months after the inauguration, Roosevelt passed away, and Truman became the nation's 33rd president. He was elected on his own merits in 1948, and the same year faced criticism with his decision that the United States should recognize the newly formed State of Israel.

During his time in office, Truman was commander in chief when the United States entered the Korean War. His legacy includes ending racial discrimination in the Armed Forces. Historians rank Truman among the "near great" presidents.

Elks Lodge #26, Kansas City, Missouri, was located in the building shown above from 1898-1951.

One of the country's oldest, Lodge #26 in Kansas City, Missouri, traces its beginnings to June 8, 1884, when it established a charter with fifteen members.

The fledgling lodge rented space at various spots around Kansas City until 1898, when members came up with a radical new idea – to purchase its own building. This was the first time that any lodge had invested in real estate – setting a precedent for other lodges.

The lodge set its sights on one of the most stunning buildings in Kansas City. Located at 7th and Grand, the imposing mansion debuted at the Chicago World's Fair in 1893 as the Wisconsin Building. Intended to reflect the natural resources of its namesake state, the 14,000 square foot building was designed by Oshkosh, Wisconsin, architect William Waters, who won a statewide contest with his design.

After the World's Fair, a Kansas City banker purchased the building and had it moved in pieces, then reconstructed at 7th and Grand. The building was home to the Wisconsin Club for several years, until Elks Lodge #26 purchased it in 1898.

The lodge held onto the building for over half a century, but decided to sell the property in 1951. The lodge moved several times during the next thirty-plus years, but in 1984 – its centennial year – built a new facility near Holmes Road and 99th.

The lodge is proud of its illustrious member Harry S. Truman, 33rd president of the United States, who became a member in 1934, eleven years before he assumed the presidency. Over the years, representatives from the Elks visited President Truman many times in the Oval Office to share with the chief executive Elks humanitarian efforts.

In 1946, representatives from the Elks presented President Truman with a report on the Order's activities to aid the country and its service personnel during WWII. Pictured above are (from left): Grand Exalted Ruler Robert S. Barrett, Past Grand Exalted Rulers Raymond Benjamin, James R. Nicholson, and David Sholtz, Grand Esquire Joseph B. Kyle, and William M. Frasor, Executive Secretary of the Elks War Commission.

John Fitzgerald Kennedy (1917-1963) was the 35th president of the United States. Elected in 1960 at age forty-three, Kennedy was at the time the youngest man who had ever assumed the office – and the first U.S. president born in the 20th century. He was a member of Elks Lodge #10 in Boston, Massachusetts.

After narrowly defeating Richard Nixon in the 1960 election, John F. Kennedy set about to impart his vision for an inspired, involved, committed America. He is credited with gaining wide support for the space race and with inspiring citizens to serve throughout the world in his brainchild, the Peace Corps.

Kennedy grew up in a wealthy, prominent Boston family and enjoyed many privileges, including world travel and education at Harvard University. When the United States entered WWII in 1941, Kennedy tried to join the Army, but was rejected for his back problems. He applied to the Navy and was accepted, serving in the South Pacific as commander of PT boats that experienced heavy combat. Kennedy was a highly decorated war hero and is credited with outstanding acts of bravery. His war experiences were the subject of a film called PT-109.

Kennedy entered politics in 1947, when he was elected representative of the 11th congressional district in Massachusetts – eventually serving three terms. He ran for U.S. Senate in 1953 and at the end of his term ran for president of the United States on the Democratic ticket. In his memorable inauguration address, he implored Americans to "ask not what your country can do for you; ask what you can do for your country." He inspired an entire generation to aspire to public service as the "best and the brightest."

The new president faced many challenges during his brief time in office – including the war in Vietnam, Civil Rights demonstrations, and the Cuban Missile Crisis. He remains one of the most popular presidents of all time for his leadership, charisma, and inspiration.

Kennedy joined Elks Lodge #10 in Boston as member 13,300.

Meeting room in Elks Lodge #10, Boston, Massachusetts

Elks Lodge #10 in Boston, Massachusetts first opened its doors in 1878, just ten years after the founding of the Order. The

Lodge's first major endeavor occurred in 1889, when members raised funds for a monument to Charles Vivian, the founder of B.P.O.E. Massachusetts Grand Lodge Trustee Willard C. Vanderlip, who traveled to Leadville, Colorado, where Charles Vivian had died, oversaw his exhumation and accompanied the body to Boston, where it was interred at Mt. Hope Cemetery and a memorial erected. Since that time, Lodge #10 has conducted an annual memorial service at the gravesite.

During WWI, the Massachusetts Elks built the first veterans' hospital in the country. Called the Elks Reconstruction Hospital, soldiers wounded in the war received specialized care for their war injuries. With more than seven hundred beds, the hospital had the facilities and staff to address the dire conditions that plagued returning veterans – including blindness that resulted from chemical warfare, disfigurement from gunshot wounds, and infection from inadequate sanitation. After three years, the Order turned over the facility to the government.

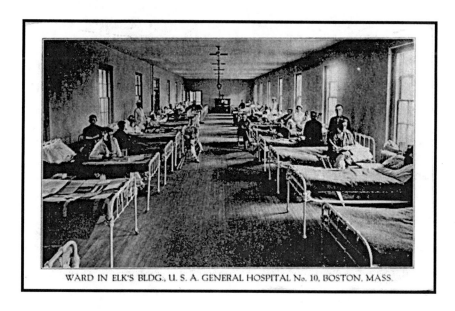

WARD IN ELK'S BLDG., U. S. A. GENERAL HOSPITAL No. 10, BOSTON, MASS.

Lodge #10 remembers with pride and pleasure that John Fitzgerald Kennedy was an active member. The lodge endeavors to develop programs that reflect the commitment to excellence, call to service, and hope for the future exemplified in President Kennedy's administration.

Gerald R. Ford

Gerald R. Ford (1913-2006) was the 38th president of the United States. In 1974, he assumed the presidency after Richard Nixon resigned as a result of the Watergate scandal. Ford's pardon of Nixon led to his loss in the 1976 election to Democrat Jimmy Carter. Many people believe that by preventing a Nixon trial, Ford sacrificed his future political career for the good of the country. When he passed away at age 93 ½, he was the country's longest living president.

In the waning years of the Nixon White House, the administration was plagued by scandal – including Vice President Spiro Agnew's indictment on felony charges for, among other crimes, accepting bribes. For his replacement, Nixon sought a man with unimpeachable character – and selected House Minority Leader, Gerald R. Ford, a twenty-five-year veteran of Congress.

Ford grew up in Grand Rapids, Michigan, and attended the University of Michigan, where he played center and linebacker for the Wolverines. His teammates voted him MVP and he was offered contracts to play professionally for the Green Bay Packers and Detroit Lions. Ford opted to coach for Yale University while attending law school. He received his law degree in 1941.

When the United States entered WWII a few months later, Ford enlisted in the U.S. Navy, where he served as a flight instructor, and later as a Lieutenant Commander on a battle ship in the South Pacific. He was the recipient of many medals and awards for his service.

After the war, Ford ran for the Congressional seat in Michigan's 5th district, which reelected him until he served as vice president and eventually president. For much of his twenty-five-year career in Congress, Ford functioned as Republican Minority Leader. It is said that he never aspired to the presidency, but did set his sights on the role of Speaker of the House.

During his two and a half years as president, Ford saw the end of America's involvement in Vietnam – a conflict that had existed for about twenty years.

During the 1976 Republican presidential primary, Ford defeated Ronald Reagan, but lost the general election to Jimmy Carter. Ford and Carter went on to establish a respectful bipartisan friendship that still serves as a model of how differing political factions can collaborate.

LODGE #48, GRAND RAPIDS, MICHIGAN

Since its inception in August 1886, Lodge #48 has been a vital part of the community in Grand Rapids, Michigan. Members have included prominent business and civic leaders, including numerous mayors as well as Congressman, and later President, Gerald R. Ford.

Elk's Club.

During the early years, the lodge rented space in various Grand Rapids buildings. In 1911, the lodge invested in a new building for the then-astronomical sum of $450,000. About fifty years later, in 1963, the lodge purchased the Grand Rapids Country Club and established operations at the facility – making adjustments and modifications to the site.

Thanks to its country club location, the lodge has hosted many golf tournaments over the years, including the PGA Seniors Tour.

Lodge #48 has always enjoyed a healthy membership base and several times has ranked as the highest-ranking in terms of membership.

Located in the heart of America, Lodge #48 is proud of its reputation as an all-American lodge and a leader in membership, facilities, and accomplishments.

The lodge is honored to count President Gerald R. Ford among its members.

Gerald R. Ford waves to the crowd during his campaign for president in 1976, America's bicentennial year.

Chapter Five
FAMOUS MEMBERS

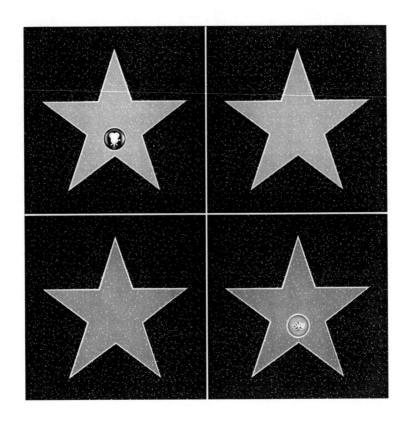

THE JOLLY CORKS FOUNDED THE ELKS TO OFFER EACH OTHER stability in their unpredictable occupations – as entertainers, they never knew when they'd be in or out of work, stranded, sick, or broke. They promised to help each other throughout their lives.

While the founders of the Elks were those who earned modest livings – when they gained regular employment at all – the Order has from its earliest days attracted celebrities and leaders in many fields.

Referring to the Elks, the *New York Times* on February 12, 1893, stated: "Nearly all of the reputable members of the theatrical profession are members, as well as prominent officials, merchants, bankers, journalists, legal and medical men, and the bright lights of America in art, literature, and music."

In this chapter, we'll visit with some of the movie stars, politicians, military heroes, sports greats, and business leaders who have been proud to call themselves Elks – or, as in the case of one actress, related to one. Our Hall of Fame even includes a well-known Western star that served as exalted ruler.

Most of the people included in the following pages are so historically significant that their images have appeared on U.S. postage stamps – now, that's famous!

Since a group of entertainers started the Elks, our notable names begin with a Hollywood superstar and the First Lady of the American Theater, then continues with other familiar show business faces. But the Elks reaches beyond entertainment – into the highest levels of political service, military rank, and sports achievements – and we'll pay homage to members from these fields as well.

CLINT EASTWOOD

Actor, Director, Producer

Elks Lodge #1285, Monterey, California

Clint Eastwood is an Oscar-winning director and producer and an Oscar-nominated actor. He began his career in television playing the now-classic character Rowdy Yates in *Rawhide*. He went on to superstar success on the big screen beginning with his star turn as the man with no name in a series of Westerns starting with *The Good, The Bad and The Ugly*. He served as mayor of Carmel, California (1986-1988), and won the Oscar for directing *Million Dollar Baby*. Eastwood joined Elks lodge #1285 in Monterey, California, near San Francisco, where he was born and raised.

HELEN HAYES

Actress

Associated with Elks Lodge #15, Washington D.C.

Helen Hayes (1900-1993) is one of only a dozen people who have won an Emmy, Grammy, Oscar, and Tony Award. She began her career at age five, and went on to enjoy unprecedented success as an actress – earning the designation as First Lady of the American Theater. President Reagan awarded her the Presidential Medal of Freedom, America's highest civilian honor. She was also the recipient of the National Medal of Arts. During an interview with Ed Sullivan in 1951, she mentioned that she owed her career to the Elks, saying: "Possibly I never would have been an actress if my father hadn't been an Elk; certainly if he hadn't been indirectly connected with the theater as chairman of the entertainment committee of his lodge in Washington. Certainly, I doubt that my mother ever could have talked him into getting us round-way tickets to New York and fifty dollars for a week there. Gee, fifty dollars was an awful lot of money in those days, but my mother was convinced that if her eight-year-old daughter could make audiences laugh in Washington, she could make them laugh on old Broadway." Hayes is pictured above with Gary Cooper in *A Farewell to Arms* (1932).

ANDY DEVINE

Actor

Exalted Ruler, Lodge #1539, San Fernando, California

Andy Devine (1905-1977) was a character actor who appeared in more than four hundred movies. When Devine came to Hollywood, people told him he'd never succeed as an actor because of his unusual squeaky voice. Devine persisted and managed to work nonstop with some of the top names in the business. He is featured prominently, along with John Wayne, in *Stagecoach*, the iconic 1939 Western directed by John Ford. Devine was an active member of Elks Lodge #1539 in San

Fernando, California, and served as Exalted Ruler in 1943. He is pictured above top with frequent costar Roy Rogers (right).

GENE AUTRY

Entertainer and Businessman

Gene Autry (1907-1998) was an actor and singer who appeared on the radio, in movies, and on television. Called "The Singing Cowboy," Autry recorded many popular tunes, but achieved his greatest acclaim with his Christmas songs, including "Frosty the Snowman," "Rudolph the Red-Nosed Reindeer," and "Here Comes Santa Claus," which he wrote. He is the only star to have five stars on the Hollywood Walk of Fame – for motion pictures, radio, recording, television, and live

theater. During WWII, he served as a pilot with the Army Air Corps, flying dangerous missions over the Himalayas. He was a successful businessman, as owner of the Los Angeles/California Angels Major League Baseball team from 1961-1997, as well as a number of television and radio stations. In 1988, he established the Museum of the American West in Los Angeles. Autry is pictured above top with Peggy Stewart in *Trail to San Antone* (1947).

JACK BENNY

Entertainer

Jack Benny (1894-1974) was a musician and comedian and a pioneer in weekly radio and television programming. An accomplished violinist, Benny started his career as a teenager accompanying vaudeville acts. He later developed a comedy routine that relied on bad violin playing and jokes about his miserly nature – which was really just an act. Benny was famous for remaining thirty-nine years old throughout his life. Bob Hope called him the "undisputed master of comic timing." Famously self-deprecating, he once answered upon receiving an award, "I don't deserve this, but I have arthritis and don't deserve that either." He has three stars on the Hollywood Walk of Fame – for radio, TV, and film. He and fellow Elk Harry S. Truman (pictured above) enjoyed a close friendship, with meetings that often included impromptu recitals.

WILL ROGERS

Entertainer

Elks Lodge #1, New York City

Will Rogers (1879-1935) was a humorist and performer on the stage and in movies. His vaudeville act consisted of him twirling a lariat and discussing topics of the day with wit and biting humor. He was an Everyman who took the side of the average man, pointing out the foibles of the rich and powerful. Part Cherokee, Rogers remarked that his family hadn't arrived on the Mayflower but was there to meet the boat. One of the most beloved celebrities of the 1920s and 1930s, Rogers was also a journalist and wrote thousands of articles for American newspapers, including the *New York Times*. His most quoted statement is "I never met a man I didn't like."

VINCE LOMBARDI

Professional Football Coach

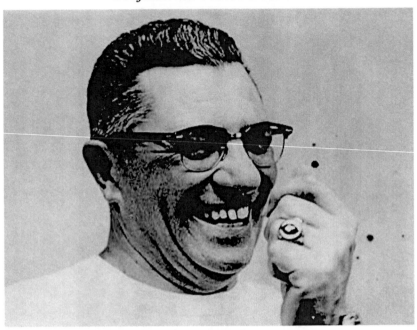

Vince Lombardi (1913-1970) was a renowned NFL football coach, most notably with the Green Bay Packers from 1959-1967 – leading the team to five NFL championships. He is widely considered the greatest coach in football history. Lombardi is also known for his motivational speaking, with many memorable quotes to his name, including: *"Winning is a habit. Watch your thoughts, they become your beliefs. Watch your beliefs, they become your words. Watch your words, they become your actions. Watch your actions, they become your habits. Watch your habits, they become your character."*

MICKEY MANTLE
Major League Baseball Player

Mickey Mantel (1931-1995) is considered one of the all-time great baseball players. He spent his entire baseball career with one team – the New York Yankees, where he played as outfielder and first baseman. Mantle has one of the most impressive records in baseball. He was named American League MVP three times, played in sixteen All Star games, participated in twelve World Series – helping his team win seven. He set World Series records for home runs, RBIs, and other feats. He has earned the designation "greatest switch hitter" in baseball, and was initiated into the National Baseball Hall of Fame in 1974.

EDDIE RICKENBACKER

Aviation Pioneer

Eddie Rickenbacker (1890-1973) was a Swiss native who served as a pilot in the American Army during WWI, earning many awards for his valor – including the nation's highest military honor, the Congressional Medal of Honor. Rickenbacker was an automotive pioneer, introducing many innovations, including four-wheel brakes, in his designs. He was also an innovator in air travel, establishing Eastern Airlines as a major service provider and heading the company for many decades.

GENERAL JOHN J. PERSHING

General of the Armies

John J. Pershing (1860-1948) graduated from West Point Academy in 1886 and subsequently served as a U.S. Army officer in six wars, most prominently during WWI, where he achieved the rank of General of the Armies. He was highly decorated for his heroism and was the recipient of the Congressional Gold Medal, the nation's highest civilian award. Pershing was considered "a general's general," and served as a

mentor to commanding generals during WWII, including Marshall, Eisenhower, Bradley, and Patton. In 1918, President Wilson allowed him to choose the day and time of WWI armistice – and Pershing chose the eleventh hour of the eleventh day of the eleventh month, a tribute to his roots in Elkdom.

JOHN BRADLEY
WWII Hero and Businessman
Elks Lodge #337, Appleton, and #662, Antigo

John Bradley (1923-1994) became an instant legend when he, along with five other soldiers, raised the U.S. flag on Mt. Suribachi, Iwo Jima, on February 23, 1945, to mark victory after one of WWII's fiercest battles. During his enlistment, Bradley served as a pharmacist's mate in the U.S. Marine Corps, earning many awards for his valor, including the Navy Cross. After the war, he went into business for himself in his hometown of Appleton, Wisconsin, and joined Elks Lodge #337 in 1945. A few years later, he moved to Antigo, Wisconsin, and joined Elks Lodge #662, where he was an active member. In 1949, Bradley appeared as himself in *Sands of Iwo Jima*, starring John Wayne. Married to his childhood sweetheart, Bradley was father to eight children, including James, who in 2000 published *Flags of Our Fathers*, a bestseller about the six men who raised the flag on Iwo Jima.

J. HERBERT KLEIN

WWII Veteran, Hollywood Producer & Entrepreneur

Elks Lodge #99, Los Angeles, and #906, Santa Monica

J. Herbert Klein (b. 1921) served in the U.S. Army Air Corps First Motion Picture Unit, an installation in Culver City, California, tasked with creating materials to train, educate, and inspire the troops during WWII. Klein reported to Captain Ronald W. Reagan, who put him in charge of initiating the unit's map program with a topographical map of California. The program evolved into one of the most top-secret projects of the war – building a topographical model of Japan and filming it from a pilot's perspective to prepare the fleet for bombing raids instrumental in ending the war. After his discharge, Klein returned to Los Angeles and headed up his family business – building luxury homes for Hollywood's elite. In 1951, he joined Elks Lodge #99 in Los Angeles and made many friends and contacts there. The same year, tycoon and movie mogul Howard Hughes tapped Klein and Charles Martin to produce his final movie – the film noir classic *Death of a Scoundrel.* Klein went on to enjoy a successful career as a producer in television, theater, and musical performance. He is the author of several memoirs as well as a biography of his mentor, Ronald Reagan.

TIP O'NEILL

Speaker of the House of Representatives

Thomas Phillip "Tip" O'Neill (1912-1994) was a congressional representative from Massachusetts for over thirty years and served as Speaker of the House of Representatives for ten years. A liberal Democrat, his larger-than-life personality and ready wit allowed him to create friendships across party lines, as evidenced by his interaction with Republican President Gerald R. Ford in the above photo. When he passed away, former President Bill Clinton remarked that he was "the nation's most prominent, powerful, and loyal champion of working people... He loved politics and government because he saw that politics and government could make a difference in people's lives. And he loved people most of all."

SAM RAYBURN

Speaker of the House of Representatives

Sam Rayburn (1882-1961) served for seventeen years as Speaker of the U.S. House of Representatives – a record. After completing law school, Rayburn was elected to the Texas House of Representatives and in 1912 as a representative for the 4th Congressional District in Texas. When he took office, Woodrow Wilson was president and, nearly fifty years later, he was still in office – during John F. Kennedy's term as president. He was serving his constituents when he died at age seventy-nine.

Chapter Six

FLAG DAY

According to Elks tradition, the purpose of the Flag Day ritual is to "honor our country's flag, to celebrate the anniversary of its birth, and to revere the achievements wrought beneath its folds."

I JOINED THE ELKS AT LODGE #99 IN LOS ANGELES ON JUNE 14, 1951 and celebrated my sixty-year anniversary on June 14, 2011 at Lodge #906 in Santa Monica, California. In both cases, I participated in a remarkable Flag Day service.

The Elks Flag Day service is truly inspiring – promoting patriotism, offering historical perspective, and creating a sense of purpose and pride.

What I love about the ritual is that it combines ceremony with celebration, song with speeches, education with inspiration. Each year, I come away from a Flag Day ceremony with a greater appreciation for both my country and my Order.

I spent many years as a manager for Big Bands throughout Southern California and can honestly say that music is my first love – so I welcome the chance to sing along with "The Star Spangled Banner," "God Bless America," and "America the Beautiful" during the ceremony. These anthems to our national identity always fill me with awe and wonder at the magnificence of our country, as symbolized in our beloved flag.

Today, we see the stars and stripes posted in front of homes, government facilities, schools, businesses – everywhere. But this wasn't always the case. It took people who believed in the power of the flag before our national banner became as ever-present as it is today.

Until the Civil War in the mid-1800s, the U.S. flag was mainly seen on government ships and forts and used to mark territory. But after the Southern states seceded from the Union and fashioned a Confederate flag, Old Glory – the flag establish-ed on June 14, 1777 – gained meaning and significance for the nation.

In the early 1860s, factories started to mass-produce the stars and stripes – a practice that, until then, had been relegated to a select few seamstresses and tailors. Once available on a large scale, U.S. flags showed up everywhere – and people were happy for the opportunity to wave the red, white, and blue and tout their love of country.

As mentioned in Chapter One, the Elks got its start a few years after the end of the Civil War, when American patriotism was at a high point – especially in Northern areas, such as New York City, where the Elks began. It's clear that the early Elks were exposed to the flag-waving patriotism that pervaded the country – and even though many of the originators of the Order were English by birth, they fell in love with their adopted home and wanted to show their appreciation for this great land.

Often, we can take the things we most value for granted – unless someone or something reminds us to stop and remember what's most important. That's what the Elks Flag Day ceremony does for me. It makes me stop and think about the liberties we enjoy, the freedoms we hold dear, and the opportunities that abound.

The flag is a symbol of America – and it's good to be reminded what it represents. As children, we learn that the thirteen stripes stand for the thirteen original colonies. But few of us recall that at one time there were fifteen stripes – two were added when Kentucky and Vermont entered the union. It finally dawned on our forefathers that they couldn't add a stripe for every new state – or else they'd end up with a flag so long it would touch the ground. It was much easier to just add a star for each state that joined the Union. And, one by one, new states came onboard until the flag sported the fifty stars we see today – and have seen since Hawaii became a state in 1959.

According to Elks history, Grand Exalted Ruler Henry A. Melvin recommended in 1907 that the Elks celebrate Flag Day and appointed a committee to prepare a Flag Day ritual by the following year.

At the Grand Lodge Session in Dallas, Texas, in 1908, the

committee presented and demonstrated the ritual – which is still in use today. Let's give thanks to our Elks brothers from the past who created our beautiful ceremony. These individuals include: James L. Kind, of Lodge #204, Topeka, Kansas; Charles B. Lahan, Lodge #4, Chicago, Illinois; and William M. Hargest of Lodge #12, Harrisburg, Pennsylvania.

The Elks was the first fraternal order – and the only one – to mandate a Flag Day observance. But the Order wanted Flag Day to achieve status throughout the nation and appealed to political leaders and elected officials. In 1916, President Woodrow Wilson responded by proclaiming June 14 as Flag Day – and encouraging communities throughout the country to find ways to honor Old Glory. In the photo at right above, noted journalist Lewis Lapham honors the flag at an Elks ceremony.

The Elks' emphasis on June 14th as Flag Day contributed to the date's eventual designation as a recognized holiday – with legislation signed in 1949 by President Harry S. Truman, a member of Elks Lodge #26 in Kansas City, Missouri.

For me, one of the high points of the Flag Day ceremony is singing "The Star Spangled Banner" along with my fellow Elks and our invited guests. There is an interesting bit of Elks history attached to this beloved song. In 1814, a young woman named Margaret Young cut the stars for a flag that flew over Fort McHenry – the same flag that inspired Francis Scott Key to write our national anthem. Margaret Young later became mother of Henry Sanderson, who was elected Grand Exalted Ruler of the

Elks in 1884.

In the Flag Day Ritual, there are many inspiring speeches and historical insights. I always enjoy hearing the Exalted Ruler proclaim: *"Our Flag is at once a history, a declaration, and a prophecy. It represents the American nation as it was at its birth: it speaks for what it is today; and it holds the opportunity for the future to add other stars to the glorious constellation."*

INVOCATION FOR DIVINE BLESSINGS
ON FLAG DAY

Almighty God, Creator and Ruler of the world, we look unto Thee in this hour of patriotic observance of the birthday of the American Flag, asking Thy blessing upon the Flag, the institutions and the people of these United States. For all that the Flag of our country represents both at home and abroad we thank Thee, and that through all our history as a nation, it has been an ensign of freedom, liberty, and opportunity, we praise Thy name, God of our fathers and our country. And through the ages yet to come may this Flag stand to all peoples over whom it may wave as the banner of liberty, freedom, and enlightenment. May this service deepen in each of us our sense of loyalty to our country and its institutions, and enable us to be better patriots, truer citizens and more loyal Americans, to Thy glory and to the honor of this great Republic. Amen.

The Flag Day service offers a wonderful opportunity to show the young people in our communities why it's important to honor the flag. I always enjoyed taking my son to the ceremonies – and while my son is now a grown man, I still enjoy taking him to the service.

Our members bring their children and grandchildren to pay tribute to Flag Day. It's heartening to see Boy Scouts serve as honor guard while we say the Pledge of Allegiance at the start of the ceremony.

During the service, we all wear small American flags on our left side, near our hearts. It's great to see the young people engage with the flag – to really examine it and study its many facets: the stars, the stripes, the red, white, and blue.

The Elks has a right to feel proud of its role in keeping the American flag on prominent display – and receiving the respect, honor, and homage it so well deserves. Well done, Elkdom!

Chapter Seven

ELEVEN O'CLOCK TOAST

In its early years, members of the Elks created a range of whimsical artwork and postcards about the Order. In this charming image, an elk and a mermaid perform the eleven o'clock toast.

As a rule, actors keep late hours – and often need time to unwind after performing. It's no wonder, then, that the charter members of the Elks held meetings that lasted late into the night – basically, this was the only time they had to socialize. At one of these late night social gatherings, the eleven o'clock toast was borne.

Some say the homage to "absent brothers" got started a few months after the Elks formally established itself as an order. Meetings were held on Sunday evenings and would last well into the late hours. Members of the Order would wait for fellow Elks to take their last curtain calls or sing their last songs and then find their way to the meeting room.

At the end of the night, members would ask each other about members who had not shown up. Had anyone seen or heard from so-and-so. Had anybody run into Tom, Dick, or Harry? Some say that as the meeting was breaking up, some of the members would polish off the refreshments, eating and drinking a share for "our absent brothers." Many entertainers had to strain to make ends meet, so this extra food and beverage was most appreciated.

George McDonald, one of the original fifteen members of the Elks, first proposed a formal toast "to our absent brothers" on May 31, 1868 – establishing the first Elks custom, one that remains a part of Elks gatherings today.

Whenever and wherever Elks are gathered, all proceedings stop at eleven, while the Exalted Ruler or a designated brother proposes the eleven o'clock toast. The tradition has evolved to include not only those who are not present at the event but also those who have passed on. In this way, Elks live on and are never really "absent" – they are always present at Elks activities, festivities, events, and celebrations.

George McDonald first proposed the eleven o'clock toast at New York Lodge #1 on May 31, 1868.

Eleven O'Clock Toast

You have heard the tolling of eleven strokes.

This is to impress upon you that with us, the hour of eleven

has a tender significance.

Wherever Elks may roam, whatever their lot in life may be,

when this hour tolls upon the dial of night, the great heart of

Elkdom swells and throbs.

It is the golden hour of recollection, the homecoming

of those who wander, the mystic roll call of those who will

come no more.

Living or dead, an Elk is never forgotten, never forsaken.

Morning and noon may pass him by, the light of day sink

heedlessly in the West, but ere the shadows of midnight shall fall,

the chimes of memory will be pealing forth the friendly message,

"To our Absent Members."

Chapter Eight

FIRST LODGES

The original altar and other furniture from New York Lodge #1 are now the proud possessions of Lodge #937 In Tallahassee, Florida. In 1912, Lewis M. Lively, Grand Esteemed Leading Knight of Lodge #937 was visiting New York Lodge #1 while it was relocating to a new facility. Lively learned that the lodge was selling its furniture to a reseller for $1,400 and offered to pay the same sum for the historic items – the first furniture designed and built for an Elks Lodge. It is estimated that the furniture dates from the earliest days of Elkdom.

WHY DID THE ELKS TAKE ROOT, THRIVE, AND FLOURISH? I believe it's because the Order was founded by entertainers that traveled from town to town and state to state. It is difficult for people today to understand how unusual it was for people to travel outside their hometown or home state back in the 1800s. These were the early days of train travel and long before the automobile arrived.

But an entertainer's livelihood depended on traveling long distances to find engagements – making the rough trips in stagecoaches, horseback, or, if lucky, locomotive.

As members of the Elks made their way to nooks and crannies, small towns, big cities, remote places, they spread the word about the Benevolent Protective Order of Elks. If the location had at least five thousand residents, a group of men within that community could apply to the Grand Lodge in New York for dispensation to start a lodge.

During the first approximately twenty years of the Elks' existence (1868-1899), the order went from one lodge in New York City to one hundred lodges from coast to coast. By 1900, there were five hundred lodges; by 1950, there were sixteen hundred lodges; and today, there are nearly three thousand lodges.

The Elks' first ten years (1868-1878) saw the formation of ten lodges – in the East (New York, Philadelphia, Baltimore, Boston), West (San Francisco, Sacramento), Midwest (Chicago, Cincinnati, St. Louis), and South (Louisville) – a stunning achievement for a young order.

In the pages that follow, we'll pay tribute to these early Elks lodges and look at some interesting facts and anecdotes about each one.

ELKS LODGES 1-50

1. NEW YORK, NY (1868)	26. KANSAS CITY, MO (1884)
2. PHILADELPHIA, PA (1871)	27. MEMPHIS, TN (1885)
3. SAN FRANCISCO, CA (1876)	28. WHEELING, WV (1885)
4. CHICAGO, IL (1876)	29. LITTLE ROCK, AK (1885)
5. CINCINNATI, OHIO (1877)	30. NEW ORLEANS, LA (1885)
6. SACRAMENTO, CA (1877)	31. SYRACUSE, NY (1886)
7. BALTIMORE, MD (1877)	32. MARION, OH (1885)
8. LOUISVILLE, KY (1877)	33. UTICA, NY (1885)
9. ST. LOUIS, MO (1878)	34. DETROIT, MI (1885)
10. BOSTON, MA (1878)	35. MERIDEN, CT (1885)
11. PITTSBURGH, PA (1878)	36. BRIDGEPORT, CT (1885)
12. CALIFORNIA (1879)	37. COLUMBUS, OH (1885)
13. INDIANAPOLIS, IN (1881)	38. NORFOLK, VA (1886)
14. PROVIDENCE, RI (1882)	39. OMAHA, NB (1886)
15. WASHINGTON, DC (1882)	40. ST. JOSEPH, MO (1886)
16. (DISSOLVED)	41. LOCKPORT, NY (1887)
17. DENVER, CO (1882)	42. LITTLE FALLS, NY (1886)
18. CLEVELAND, OH (1883)	43. ADRIAN, MI (1886)
19. HARTFORD, CT (1883)	44. MINNEAPOLIS, MN (1886)
20. PEORIA, IL (1883)	45. RICHMOND, VA (1886)
21. NEWARK, NJ (1883	46. MILWAUKEE, WI (1886)
22. BROOKLYN, NY (1883)	47. EAST SAGINAW, MI (1886)
23, BUFFALO, NY (1884)	48. GRAND RAPIDS, MI (1886)
24. ROCHESTER, NY (1885)	49. ALBANY, NY (1886)
25. NEW HAVEN, CT (1884)	50. KALAMAZOO, MI (1887)

ELKS LODGES 51-100

51. SPRINGFIELD, OH (1886)	76. DELAWARE, OH (1888)
52. CHILLICOTHE, OH (1887)	77. CIRCLEVILLE, OH (1888)
53. TOLEDO, OH (1886)	78. ATLANTA, GA (1888)
54. LIMA, OH (1887)	79. BIRMINGHAM, AL (1889)
55. CINCINNATI, OHIO (1886)	80. LINCOLN, NE (1888)
56. YOUNGSTOWN, OH (1886)	81. GLENS FALLS, NY (1888)
57. MANSFIELD, OH (1886)	82. PORTSMOUTH, VA (1888)
58. DAYTON, OH (1886)	83. UPPER SANDUSKY, OH (1888)
59. ST. PAUL, MN (1887)	84. BURLINGTON, IA (1888)
60. PATTERSON, NJ (1887)	85. SALT LAKE CITY, UT (1888)
61. SPRINGFIELD, MA (1887)	86. TERRE HAUTE, IN (1888)
62. ELMIRA, NY (1887)	87. LOWELL, MA (1889)
63. CUMBERLAND, MD (1887)	88. BAY CITY, MI (1889)
64. ROCKFORD, IL (1887)	89. LEXINGTON, KY (1888)
65. LAWRENCE, MA (1887)	90. PUEBLO, CO (1888)
66. LOGANSPORT, IN (1887)	91. CHATTANOOGA, TN (1888)
67. ERIE, PA (1888)	92. SEATTLE, WA (1888)
68. CANTON, OH (1887)	93. HAMILTON, OH (1888)
69. NEW CASTLE, PA (1887)	94. TIFFIN, OH (1889)
70. BINGHAMTON, NY (1888)	95. VICKSBURG, MS (1888)
71. DALLAS, TX (1888)	96. ROME, NY (1888)
72. NASHVILLE, TN (1887)	97. PORTSMOUTH, NH (1888)
73. NEW BEDFORD, MA (1887)	98. DES MOINES, IA (1889)
74. HOBOKEN, NJ (1888)	99. LOS ANGELES, CA (1889)
75. FINDLAY, OH (1888)	100. QUINCY, IL (1889)

LODGE #1, NEW YORK CITY, NEW YORK
ESTABLISHED 1868

New York Lodge #1 celebrated its 66th anniversary in 1934 with special guests that included Mayor Fiorello LaGuardia (front row, left) and Governor Al Smith (front row, right).

NEW HOME

NEW YORK LODGE No. 1

200 Rooms with Baths

Restaurant, Grill Room, Bowling, Billiards, Pool, Library, Lounging and Waiting Rooms

43rd Street, near Broadway

VISITORS ALWAYS WELCOME

The largest and most beautiful Lodge Room in the world

In 1912, Lodge #1 moved into a new home at 43rd Street, near Broadway.

LODGE #2, PHILADELPHIA, PENNSYLVANIA
ESTABLISHED 1871

The vintage postcard above shows Philadelphia Lodge #2 along with an inset photo of the lodge's exalted ruler. The matchbook at right, probably from the 1930s, shows elegant people enjoying an evening at the Philadelphia lodge.

Early members of the Elks included many composers, who created original songs for the lodges. The above image shows the sheet music for "Elk March" written by J.S. Cox, who dedicated the song to Philadelphia Lodge #2.

LODGE #3, SAN FRANCISCO, CALIFORNIA
ESTABLISHED 1876

San Francisco Lodge #3 is the oldest continuously operating lodge in Elkdom. Its current building at 450 Post Street was commissioned by the lodge in the early 1920s and completed in 1925. The lodge continues to thrive with over one thousand members.

San Francisco Lodge #3 features a magnificent swimming pool, where Olympian Mark Spitz (pictured below) swam as a child – because his grandfather was a member.

LODGE #4, CHICAGO, ILLINOIS
ESTABLISHED 1876

This photo from the *Chicago Daily News* archive shows Chicago Lodge #4 during the early 1900s. The address is listed at 174 W. Washington.

LODGE #5, CINCINNATI, OHIO
ESTABLISHED 1877

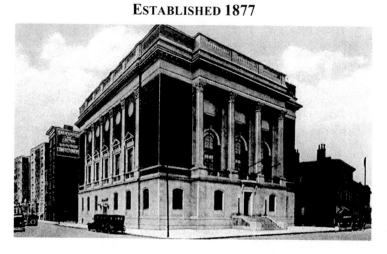

The above postcard from the 1920s shows Cincinnati Elks Lodge #5 at 9th and Elm. Decades later, the building became the home of a local television station.

Like many Elks lodges, the Cincinnati lodge featured customized fine china.

LODGE #6, SACRAMENTO, CALIFORNIA
ESTABLISHED 1877

The Elks Building at 921 11th Street was dedicated in 1926.

Sacramento Elks Lodge #6 boasts a colorful history, which includes an in-house band featuring the vintage drums pictured at right. (Photo by Lance Armstrong/The Pocket News)

Anthony M. Muljat has been a member of Sacramento Lodge #6 for over sixty-five years and has served as lodge treasurer. (Photo by Lance Armstrong/The Pocket News)

LODGE #7, BALTIMORE, MARYLAND

ESTABLISHED 1877

In 1916, the Elks held its annual Grand Lodge Session in Baltimore and celebrated with a festive, all-American parade.

LODGE #8, LOUISVILLE, KENTUCKY
ESTABLISHED 1877

LODGE #9, ST. LOUIS, MISSOURI
ESTABLISHED 1878

Louisville Lodge #8 and St. Louis Lodge #9 created similar postcards to display their range of facilities.

Lodge #10, Boston, Massachusetts
Established 1878

In the early 1900s, Boston Lodge #10 established a hotel at 275 Tremont Street.

Chapter Nine

ELKS NATIONAL HOME

The Elks National Home is a retirement community located in Bedford, Virginia, that houses approximately one hundred members.

BY THE TURN OF THE TWENTIETH CENTURY, THE ELKS HAD grown to six hundred lodges with seventy-five thousand members. In thirty-two years, from the Order's founding in 1868 until 1900, the Elks had become a major force in American life – influencing culture, social life, politics, and charitable works. As the Order aged, so did its members. By 1900, many Elks were well into their seventies and eighties – and the Order decided to build a national home where members could live out their retirement.

In 1902, a committee located a property in Bedford, Virginia, that seemed perfect – a large hotel situated on over one hundred acres of beautiful land at the eastern base of the Blue Ridge Mountains. The Elks placed the winning bid on the property during an auction, and within a year the Elks National Home was in operation.

A decade later, the home was in such demand that the Elks decided to expand the facilities. After several expansions, the Order began construction on a new building – one that was more

spacious and up-to-date than the existing hotel.

On July 8, 1916, the Elks celebrated its new National Home with a dedication ceremony attended by members from throughout the nation as well as luminaries from all walks of life. A special guest was Senator, later President, Warren G. Harding – a member of Elks Lodge #32 in Marion, Ohio. He is pictured above during the dedication ceremony.

The photo above shows the original Elks National Home, formerly the Hotel Bedford, which the Order purchased at a bankruptcy auction in 1902. The successful negotiations for the property was largely due to the efforts of Meade Detweiler, Grand Exalted Ruler (1895, 1896, 1897), pictured at right. A lawyer by profession, Detweiler enjoyed a successful career and was known for his kind heart and good works. It is said that he elevated the Elks to heights of "brilliancy and usefulness."

Dedication Program

MUSIC—Reverie "Wayside Chapel" . . . . . . Roanoke Machine Works Band

Invocation . . . . Rev. Dallas Tucker
Portsmouth, O., No. 134

Address of Welcome . . . . Hon. J. Lawrence Campbell
Mayor of Bedford City, Va.

MUSIC—Potpourri "Sweet Old Songs" . . . . Band

Address . . . . Hon. A. J. Montague
Richmond, Va., No. 45 (Governor of Virginia)

Address . . . . Hon. John W. Daniel
Lynchburg, Va., No. 321 (United States Senator)

Address . . . . Frederick Warde
St. Louis, Mo., No. 9

MUSIC—Fantasia "Grand Americus" . . . . Band

Transfer of Building to B. P. O. Elks . . . . Joseph T. Fanning
Indianapolis, Ind., No. 13 (Chairman Board of Grand Trustees)

Acceptance of Building . . . . George P. Cronk
Omaha, Neb., No. 39 (Grand Exalted Ruler)

MUSIC—Overture "William Tell" . . . . Band

Oration . . . . Meade D. Detweiler
San Francisco, Cal., No. 3 (Chairman Home Committee)

Benediction . . . . Rev. John D. Boland
Baltimore, Md., No. 7

Hymn—"Auld Lang Syne"

The Elks National Home was dedicated on May 21, 1903. Over five thousand Elks from across the country attended the ceremony in Bedford, Virginia. In the above photo, Meade Detweiler salutes the gathering after delivering his dedication address.

The above photo (on this and the facing page) from the Library of Congress collection was taken by Waller Holladay in 1916, when the new building for the Elks National Home was completed.

The Elks National Home was not and is not intended as a charitable institution or a nursing home. It is a retirement community, where members of the Order can live out their days in friendship and among the society of fellow Elks.

During over a century in operation, the Elks National Home has welcomed four thousand occupants – with a high percentage of veterans. For years, the home has had a waiting list – and an applicant's lodge must recommend the individual for acceptance.

Today, approximately one hundred people – men and women – reside at the Elks National Home, appreciating the opportunity to, as the motto states, "retire among friends."

The slogan of the Elks National Home is "Retire Among Friends."

Chapter Ten
ELKS MEMORIAL

The Elks Memorial in Chicago, Illinois, was officially dedicated in 1926 as a tribute to the Elks who had given their lives fighting in WWI. The Elks rededicated the building in 1946 to honor the Elks who had perished during WWII.

PRESIDENT WOODROW WILSON CALLED IT "THE WAR TO END all wars." Today, we refer to the conflict as World War I, but at the time people referred to it as The Great War. After the war ended, people wanted to believe the world would enjoy lasting peace. This was one of the reasons the Elks decided to build a National Veterans Memorial. The Order wished to honor the seventy thousand Elks who served during the war and pay special tribute to the sacrifices made by one thousand members who gave their lives fighting oppression in Europe. In all, nearly twenty million people from both sides of the conflict died during over four years of fighting (1914-1918).

To honor its fallen members, the Elks wanted to construct a beautiful, grand edifice that would stand the test of time – and compare with the most awe-inspiring structures on the planet. To this end, the Order asked seven of the finest architects in the United States to submit designs for an Elks Veterans Memorial and National Headquarters.

The winning entry came from Egerton Swarthout for a design deemed beautiful and classic as well as practical and efficient. Construction began during 1923 and the cornerstone was laid on June 7, 1924. Two years later, the building was officially dedicated during the Elks Grand Lodge Reunion. In creating the monument, the Elks' objective was to memorialize those who perished in the war and to inspire feelings of patriotism and pride in all who viewed the structure.

When war again erupted in Europe during 1939, the conflict was called World War II. After Japan's attack on Pearl Harbor in December 1941, the United States entered the fighting and remained until the war's end in August 1945. After the war, the Elks wanted to honor the valorous service of its one hundred thousand members who served and nearly two thousand members who died during the conflict and rededicated the Elks National Memorial on September 8, 1946.

Construction on the building began in 1923 and was completed the following year. The above photo shows the center dome under construction with Lincoln Park and Lake Michigan in the background.

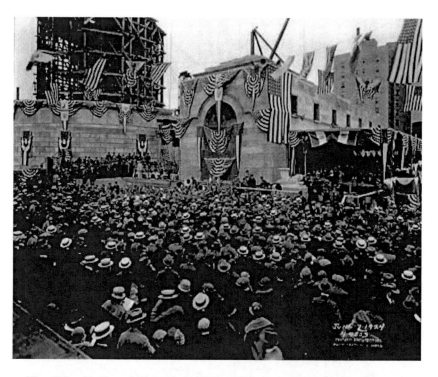

The Elks National Veterans Memorial was officially dedicated on July 14, 1926, during the Order's Grand Lodge Reunion.

The building's rotunda is reminiscent of classic revival memorials such as those dedicated to Abraham Lincoln and Thomas Jefferson.

Architecture writers have compared the reception hall in the Elks Memorial to rooms in European palaces.

The Elks Memorial stands in one of Chicago's most exclusive areas, with a broad view of Lincoln Park and just a short distance from Lake Michigan.

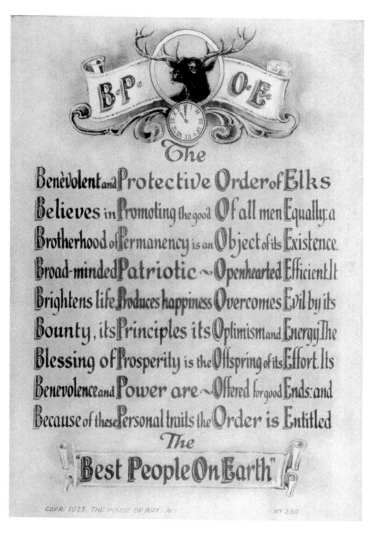

The Elks National Veterans Memorial is just one reason why many people believe that B.P.O.E. stands for Best People on Earth.

Chapter Eleven

MEMORIAL SERVICES

Elks Memorial Day takes place each year on the first Sunday of December. At that time, members of the lodge honor their absent brothers – and, since 1995, sisters.

AT THE GRAND LODGE SESSION IN 1890, THE ELKS ADOPTED A new constitution and new statute that read: *"The first Sunday in December of each year is hereby designated and dedicated as a day on which shall be commemorated by every Lodge of Elks, the memorial of our departed Brothers and shall be known as The Elks Memorial Day."*

Since that time, the Elks have dedicated the first Sunday in the last month of the year to commemorate members of the lodge who passed away the previous year. The Order's beautiful, moving ritual honors the departed and reminds the living to value life – and realize that someday all members will be together again.

During the ritual, the Exalted Ruler recites these inspiring words before directing the Secretary to call the roll of the absent:

"...Firm in our faith, we are reminded by these services that we are born, not to die, but to live. True, the light of beloved eyes has faded from our sight, but it shines more brightly upon another shore. Voices we loved to hear at the fireside, in the marts of trade, or in fraternal association, are silenced, but they will live again in the music of the Choir Invisible, and blend forever in the harmony of angels. Memorial Day with us is a day of tender sentiment. Hope dries our tears, and with eyes of faith we may see those whom we have loved and lost awhile, faring on through a better land awaiting the day when the chain of fraternal love shall be reunited forevermore."

At the close of the ceremony, which includes the singing of "Auld Lang Syne," the Exalted Ruler tells the gathering: "In renewing our fidelity to the memory of our departed brothers, may we be inspired ever to a life of service to the living. And may the Grace of the Grand Exalted Ruler of All enable us to derive from this ceremony renewed confidence that beyond the shadows there is life everlasting."

Auld Lang Syne

Should auld ac-quain-tance be for-got and ne-ver brought to mind? Should auld ac-quain-tance be for-got And days o' auld lang syne. For auld lang syne, my dear, For auld lang syne, We'll drink a cup o' kind-ness yet For auld lang syne.

The Elks Memorial ceremony usually includes participants singing "Auld Lang Syne" in honor of departed brothers and sisters. The lyrics were written by Scots poet Robert Burns in 1788. The title words loosely mean "for the sake of old times."

MEMORIAL SERVICE

Over the years, programs for the annual Elks Memorial Service have included beautiful artwork that includes the words "cervus alces," the Latin name for elk.

B·P·O·E·

"The faults of our brothers we write upon the sands
Their virtues on the tablets of love and memory."

THE ELK

An Elk is a jolly good fellow,
  An Apostle of Good-Will and Cheer,
For his is the Creed of Unselfishness
  Every day of every year;
His spirit of Charity is one that lifts
  In a quiet helpful way.
    His Brotherly Love
  Is to aid however he may.

An Elk is an Apostle of Sunshine,
  Beyond a doubt this is true,
For he practices "Do unto others"
  As you'd have them do unto you."

© JOHN DREXCHER CO. Inc. N·Y.   H.H. Fariss.

Many poets have been inspired to pen tributes to fellow Elks. Included above is a poem entitled "The Elk" by H.H. Fariss.

Many songwriters have composed tunes dedicated to departed members of the Elks. These songs include "The Chimes of Eleven" by Joseph Carey, as shown in the cover of the sheet music above.

Chapter Twelve
ELKS MAGAZINE

The June 1933 issue of *The Elks Magazine* took readers on a tour of the Chicago World's Fair. The edition marked the eleventh anniversary of the magazine.

BY THE EARLY 1920s, ELKS MEMBERSHIP EXCEEDED EIGHT hundred thousand – and, as the membership increased, so did the difficulty of trying to communicate between the Grand Lodge and subordinate lodges.

Up to this point, Elks headquarters had three basic ways of communicating with the other lodges. First of all, a delegate from the lodge would attend the annual Grand Lodge meeting and report what he'd heard to the home lodge. The second method of communication was official letters from the Grand Exalted Ruler sent to the lodges and read during meetings. The third type of communication occurred through newsletters and other publications issued on an individual lodge level.

The problems with these forms of communication were many and varied. With close to a million members, the Grand Lodge had no way of knowing how many people would show up at meetings to hear reports or letters. While the newsletters from individual lodges were well meaning, many did not reflect the high standards of the Elks – and since these were issued by just a few lodges, they did not have a significant impact on communication.

To address these concerns, the Elks decided to issue a monthly journal called *The Elks Magazine* – mandating a publication of the highest quality in terms of literary and artistic merit comparable to the best magazines of the day.

The Elks Magazine was initiated as a way to disseminate consistent information to all members of the Elks – and to deliver content that was educational, informative, and entertaining. As part of membership, each Elk received a subscription to the magazine. With an initial circulation of nearly one million, *The Elks Magazine* became one of the leading publications in America.

The Elks Magazine

Volume One   *Magazine*   Number One

Features *for* June, 1922

NATIONAL PUBLICATION OF THE BENEVOLENT AND PROTECTIVE ORDER OF ELKS OF THE UNITED STATES OF AMERICA

Published Under the Direction of the Elks National Memorial Headquarters Commission: John K. Tener, *Chairman;* Joseph T. Fanning, *Secretary-Treasurer;* James R. Nicholson, Edward Rightor, Fred Harper, Bruce A. Campbell, William M. Abbott, Rush L. Holland, Frank L. Rain, William W. Mountain, Grand Exalted Ruler (Ex-Officio)

50 East 42nd Street   New York City

Joseph T. Fanning, *Executive Director*
Robert W. Brown, *Editor*   Charles S. Hart, *Business Manager*

The Elks Magazine is published monthly at 50 East 42nd Street, New York City, by the Benevolent and Protective Order of Elks, U. S. A. Entry as second-class matter applied for at the Post-office, New York, N. Y., under the act of March 3d, 1879. Single copy, price 20 cents. Subscription price in the United States and Possessions, for Non-Elks, $2.00 a year; for Elks, $1.00 a year. For postage to Canada add 50 cents; for foreign postage add $1.00. Subscriptions are payable in advance. In ordering change of address please allow four weeks' time, and give both old and new addresses. The Editors cannot undertake to return unsolicited contributions, unless there be accompanied by stamped self-addressed envelopes.

The Table of Contents for *The Elks Magazine*'s first issue in June 1922 featured a range of articles, stories, and features – including a letter from President Warren G. Harding.

DEAR BROTHER ELKS:—

Now arrives The Elks Magazine, and out of a heart deeply stirred with pride in the achievement, and with foreknowledge of the success in store, I am privileged as Grand Exalted Ruler to offer my congratulations to the Order at large.

The Elks Magazine establishes an advanced era in our fraternal progress and development. It invests us with a new and powerful element of strength and another instrumentality by which to translate and concrete opportunity in the practical results of our planning and organizing and of our leadership along the upward way. With its riches of information, its wholesome and stimulating intellectual entertainment, it stands pledged to place before its audience the first of every month the finest magazine published. It will be guided and controlled by a fixed policy that the best there is belongs by divine right and is dedicated to our great and growing fellowship.

That which pleases and gratifies me most of all is the fact that The Elks Magazine is YOUR Magazine — yours in the point of personal possession and proprietorship. It speaks and stands for your sentiments and your principles. It does honor to our Flag. It preaches and it practises the reality of Brotherly Love. I would impress the thought that a primary function will be to keep you enlightened and alive as to the ambitions of the Order expressive of its highest estate, and of its wide-reaching activities in carrying forward these ambitions.

As Grand Exalted Ruler, and thereby as a member of the Elks National Memorial Headquarters Commission, and having actively participated in the foundation work for the establishment of The Elks Magazine, I cheerfully bear witness to the vigilant care that has dominated with business prudence every successive step forward, and that now culminates in its delivery into your hands.

In the multitude and talent and experience from which we are able to draw, and in the array of so many gifted minds, it is to be expected and it is requested that many among our members will be inspired to volunteer their suggestions alike for editorial and publication features of attraction and improvement. I am assured by those in charge that the doors of The Elks Magazine will stand wide open to welcome new ideas intended for its good. Out of such close co-operation and mutual dependence, following these lead lines, and in the exercise and administration of our joint proprietorship, there can come only substantial betterment and a larger prosperity.

It goes without mentioning that The Elks Magazine will be worth considerably more than the nominal price named for subscription, which is after all, in easy analysis, one more tribute to your good fortune in being a member of our Order.

The beginning is first-class. The augury is for better and better as time comes and goes. From the light of the past, we look optimistically into the future, and we have cause to congratulate ourselves and each other. In all sincerity, I bespeak and commend your welcome.

W. W. Mountain

Grand Exalted Ruler.

In the inaugural issue of *The Elks Magazine*, Grand Exalted Ruler William W. Mountain outlined the Order's objectives for the new publication, including that it educate, inform, and entertain readers and deliver content of the highest excellence.

During the early 1930s, a group of Elks traveled from Chicago, Illinois, to Birmingham, Alabama – and parts in between – in a Studebaker convertible on a goodwill tour for *The Elks Magazine*. The men are pictured here in Cedar Rapids, Iowa, on June 3, 1932.

YOUR LODGE WILL BE PROUD OF BOYS LIKE THESE!
THEY WILL TRAIN AS A UNIT IN UNCLE SAM'S ARMY!
SEND AN AVIATION GROUP LIKE THIS FROM YOUR HOME TOWN!

ELKS LODGES throughout America are successfully instituting refresher courses in cooperation with local educational authorities. They are helping ambitious young men to pass necessary mental examinations for aviation cadets in the world's finest air corps.

The Elks National Defense Commission has already furnished information to all subordinate lodges. This is also available at every Army Recruiting Station.

A college degree is not required . . . high school graduates can "bone up" through refresher courses instituted by Elks lodges.

An Elks unit of twenty young men—all friends and neighbors—will train together. A lesser number of can-

didates can join another nearby Elks lodge unit. They share the work, fun and friendly rivalry during the training period . . . $75 a month—plus uniforms, board, lodging, medical care and $10,000 insurance—during the seven and a half months they are learning.

Up to $245.50 a month when commissioned a Second Lieutenant; $150 allowance for initial officer's uniform equipment, and, when returned to civil life, a $500 cash bonus for each year of active service under a reserve commission!

HAS YOUR LODGE DONE ITS PART?

"KEEP 'EM FLYING"

ELKS NATIONAL DEFENSE COMMISSION.

36

This public service message appeared in *The Elks Magazine* during December 1941 – the month that the United States entered WWII. The ad is recruiting Elks to join the U.S. Army as aviation cadets.

Chapter Thirteen
ELKS NATIONAL FOUNDATION

Each year, the Elks National Foundation awards millions of
dollars in scholarships to outstanding students.

To FURTHER THE ORDER'S CHARITABLE, EDUCATIONAL, AND patriotic aims, the B.P.O.E. Grand Lodge in 1928 established the Elks National Foundation with seed money of one hundred thousand dollars. Since that time, additional funds have come from individual members, lodges, state associations, and other citizens and organizations.

Through its outreach efforts, the Elks National Foundation is endeavoring to build better communities, where worthy young people get educational opportunities, veterans receive the care and respect they deserve, children and teens are shown how to resist peer pressure related to drugs, and girls and boys can take part in activities that encourage good sportsmanship and strength of character.

The foundation awards millions each year to these outreach programs, which touch every corner of America. In this way, the Elks National Foundation is doing its part to help create happy, healthy, well-balanced communities by providing opportunities to people who need and deserve a chance to succeed.

The Elks National Foundation sponsors a myriad of programs for veterans, providing assistance to wounded veterans and support to members of the National Guard. One of the foundation's most innovative programs is Adopt-A-Vet, where individual members and lodges adopt veterans, visiting them on holidays and other special occasions, treating the veterans to dinners and gifts. The foundation also supplies leather to veterans' hospitals for occupational therapy, where the vets make belts, wallets, and moccasins for later sale at Elks-sponsored art fairs.

The Elks National Foundation invests nearly a million annually in drug awareness programs, including a collaboration with Marvel Comics and the U.S. government's Substance Abuse and Mental Health Services Administration. In a comic book called *Hard Choices*, Spiderman and the Fantastic Four, along with Elroy the Elk, show kids in fourth through eighth grades the dangers of underage drinking.

The National Elks Foundation initiated Hoop Shoot during the 1970s. Since that time, it has become one of the country's premier sporting activities for grammar school and middle school boys and girls in communities across the country.

Chapter Fourteen
ELKS EVOLVING

Members of Lodge #2790 (Van Nuys-Reseda, California) elected Tiffany Lace exalted ruler in 2011 when she was just twenty-four — making her one of the youngest exalted rulers in the United States. In a *Los Angeles Daily News* article, she was called "an inspiration for a whole new generation of Elks."
(Photo by Hans Gutknecht, *Los Angeles Daily News*)

As of this writing, the B.P.O.E. has nearly one million members in close to three thousand lodges – and the challenge is for the Order to keep growing and attracting new members, especially those from the younger generations.

The Elks has evolved with the times – and is no longer an exclusive men's-only organization The Order welcomes people of all races, creeds, and nationalities, and in 1995 opened membership to women.

The Elks can be proud of its diverse, inclusive membership – this is one of the reasons our Order will remain vital and strong. By making ourselves significant – even indispensable – in our communities, people will want to join with us.

It's exciting to learn how lodges around the country are attracting new members through membership drives, open houses, community involvement, and other forms of outreach. The past five years has seen some major growth in the Order's membership.

An article in the March 15, 2006 edition of *USA Today* was a boon for our Order, explaining how the twenty- and thirty-somethings are discovering the Elks. The article mentions a "social insurgency sweeping through medium-size boomtown cities and suburbs across the nation: young professionals joining the Benevolent and Protective Order of Elks." In many lodges across the country, the majority of members are under forty – notably Denver, Detroit, San Francisco, Austin (Texas), and Hoboken (New Jersey).

On April 19, 2006, an article appeared in the *Southern Maryland Enterprise* that discusses how St. Mary's Lodge #2092 in Maryland is "riding the wave of a new generation of members," and that "opening to women nationwide...helped boost membership and allowed the lodges to become more family-friendly." At the time of the article, Lodge #2092 had just elected its first woman exalted ruler, Pamela Lentz.

A *Los Angeles Daily News* article on May 27, 2011 told the story of Tiffany Lace, who, at age twenty-four, became one of the youngest exalted rulers in the country. Exalted Ruler Lace leads Van Nuys-Reseda Lodge #2790 in Southern California. Active in the local community, with a career as a grammar school math teacher, two of her sisters also belong to the lodge. She feels it is her mission to attract younger members to the Order and has developed a range of programs to capture the community's imagination and attention – including murder mystery dinners, casino nights, and holiday parties.

In Summit, New Jersey, Lois Pagano was elected exalted ruler of Lodge #1246 in 2011 – the lodge's centennial year. During her six years as an Elk, Exalted Ruler Pagano has seen membership grow from one hundred and fifty members to seven hundred and fifty members – a 500% increase! She attributes this phenomenal growth to word of mouth – people in the community attend an open house or other event at the lodge and spread the news. Many of the new members are parents with young children and women in their thirties. The lodge raises community aware-ness of their activities through an ongoing public relations campaign that communicates, as Pagano says, "that the Elks is the country's premier charitable organization."

Members of Lodge #1246 in Summit, New Jersey, elected Lois Pagano Exalted Ruler in 2011. She is the first woman to serve in this capacity in the lodge's one hundred year history. (Photo by Aristide Economopoulos/*The Star-Ledger*, Newark, NJ)

Bob Wright served as exalted ruler of Lodge #290 in Waterloo, Iowa in the 2005-2006 term. He was the first African American elected to that office.

During the 1970s, Bob Wright joined Lodge #290 in Waterloo, Iowa, where he was active in the community as a teacher, coach, guidance counselor, assistant principal, and principal. Lodge #290 got its start in 1894 and in 1924 moved to a now-historic building at 407 E. Park Avenue. The lodge has always enjoyed a thriving membership and has remained an integral part of the community. Members of Lodge #290 elected Bob Wright as exalted ruler in 2005. During his tenure, the lodge raised contributions toward repairs for its aging facility. In 2008, the lodge completed the two-million-dollar renovations – and gained funds for the repairs from throughout the community.

In 2011, the Elks achieved a first – a mother and daughter elected as exalted rulers during the same year. In the photo at left, Patricia Mullin (left), exalted ruler of Lodge #286 in Ocala, Florida, and Bonnie Mullin (right), exalted ruler of Lodge #25 in New Haven, Connecticut, enjoy their mutual accomplishment. Both mother and daughter are committed to increasing membership in their lodges.

In 2011, Susan Albertoni, (right) an attorney in Merced, California, became the first woman elected as exalted ruler in the history of Lodge #1240 (Merced). She joined the lodge because of its commitment to charitable endeavors and community service and the work it does with youth organizations.

George Aguilar, Jr., (left), past exalted ruler of Lodge #2379 in Santa Clarita, California, with his father George Aguilar, Sr., past exalted ruler of Lodge #2790 in Van Nuys, California.

In 2009, George Aguilar, Jr., became exalted ruler of Lodge #2379 in Santa Clarita, California. He was the first Hispanic American elected to this office. Leadership runs in the family because his father, George Aguilar, Sr., served as exalted ruler of Lodge #2790 in Van Nuys, California.

These individuals and many others prove that the B.P.O.E. is a vital and vibrant organization that continues to grow, evolve, and change – for the better.

Another way B.P.O.E. keeps up with the times is finding new ways to communicate. The original fifteen members easily shared ideas across a small room at 17 Delancey Street, and modern technology allows today's membership of nearly a million to feel just as connected.

Andy Costello, public relations chairman of the California-Hawaii Elks Association, has made it his mission to promote fast, easy interaction among one hundred and seventy-five lodges in his association. To this end, he has encouraged members to serve on the public relations committees of their lodges and use up-to-date methods and innovative concepts to inform members of the Elks – as well as people in their communities – about local activities and benevolent programs.

Andy Costello joined B.P.O.E. in 1980 and is a member of Mission Viejo Saddleback Valley Lodge #2444, where he has been an officer and lodge organist for three decades. Costello served as lodge public relations chairman for ten years and Orange Coast District public relations chairman for five years. In 2009, he began multi-year service as California-Hawaii Elks Association public relations chairman responsible for overseeing the PR activities of California and Hawaii lodges.

Lodges that create their own websites, email electronic newsletters to members, and contact on-line media in their communities are highly effective in not only communicating Elks news – but also in attracting new members, mainly computer-literate men and women under forty with families.

The Elks Grand Lodge also offers a comprehensive website to keep members well informed, inspired, and motivated – and provides an overview of the Order, its history, and activities for people interested in joining.

B.P.O.E. will continue to embrace positive change, while maintaining its cherished, time-honored traditions – staying in touch with its rich history while keeping pace with society's rapid advancements.

Chapter Fifteen

STARS OF TOMORROW

Stars of Tomorrow is my suggestion for a high school talent competition sponsored by Elks lodges. The competition would take place on local, statewide, and nationwide levels. I believe the program could attract a whole new generation of members to the Order.

ONE OF MY BEST EXPERIENCES WITH THE ELKS OCCURRED IN 1968, when I produced the First Annual American Theatre Awards – a gala event attended by about eighteen hundred Hollywood professionals. With Pat Boone and Maureen O'Hara as hosts and industry notables, including director Robert Wise, as talent judges, the evening had the glitz and glamour of the Academy Awards combined with a high-minded, serious purpose – to give aspiring actors exposure, while making exciting new talent available to the industry. The evening was the culmination of an Elks-sponsored talent competition in California colleges and universities.

During the evening, young, undiscovered actors performed prepared scenes, which alternated with performances by established comedians, singers, and dancers. At the conclusion, the judges selected a winning actor and actress who were presented with trophies – and granted scholarships and screen tests.

The winning actor, Eric Server, went on to enjoy a lengthy career, mainly in television – with roles in top programs such as *Mission Impossible, The Incredible Hulk, The A-Team, Dynasty,* and *Star Trek.* During his career, Eric has appeared in nearly a hundred TV episodes.

Eric Server in a scene from *The Incredible Hulk* (1980).

I'm happy to report that after more than forty years, I've reconnected with Eric – a fine actor and wonderful human being – and we're now in discussions about several projects where he'd serve as producer.

In March 1968, I produced the 1st Annual American Theatre Awards, a live show hosted by singer Pat Boone and actress Maureen O'Hara. The event gave new talent a chance to shine – and get discovered.

190

The objective of the American Theatre Awards is to seek out in Universities, Colleges, and Dramatic Schools, the most talented young people in the field of dramatic arts, all of whom are non-professional, and give them the opportunity to be seen and heard by respected professionals of stage, screen and television.

Through their sponsors, the Benevolent and Protective Order of Elks, the American Theatre Awards will hold future acting competition in every state. Winners of the individual state awards will then compete on a national level and these winners will be awarded scholarships and screen tests.

Through the American Theatre Awards, the aspiring young actor gets valuable exposure, plus the opportunity to advance in his chosen profession. At the same time, a fresh source of exciting new talent is made available to motion pictures, television and the stage.

•◦•

JUDGES

MR. ROBERT WISE	Producer, 20th Century Fox Studio
MR. AL TRESCONY	Director of Talent, M.G.M. Studios
MR. JACK CUMMINGS	Independent Producer
MR. JAMES DOOLITTLE	General Director, Greek Theatre Assn.
MR. JACK ROBERTS	Director of Talent, Warner Bros. - 7 Arts Studio
MR. CURT CONWAY	Director of Talent, 20th Century Fox Studio
MISS MAY MANN	Movie Columnist
MR. SOL BAER FIELDING	Independent Producer
MISS PATTI MOORE	Comedienne
DR. JAMES H. BUTLER	Chairman, Div. of Drama, U.S.C., and National President of American Educational Theatrical Assn

•◦•

PRESENTERS OF AWARDS
MISS JULIE PARRISH
MR. JAMES MacARTHUR
YVONNE CRAIG
MR. YALE SUMMERS
MISS MARILYN MAXWELL

Judges at the Elks-sponsored 1st Annual American Theatre Awards included my best friend, May Mann, and multiple Academy Award winner Robert Wise, director of *West Side Story* and *The Sound of Music*.

PROGRAM

JOE HOUSER
Vice President California · Hawaii Elks Association

LOU ALEXANDER
Comedian

PAT BOONE   MAUREEN O'HARA
Introduction of Judges

PAT BOONE   Introduction of First Act

UNIVERSITY OF CALIFORNIA AT LOS ANGELES
Scene · "The Lark";   Actors · Bob Carricart Jr. & Judy Kaye

MAUREEN O'HARA   Introduction to:
Mario Lanza Memorial Award

MARK RICHARDSON   (Sings)
"My Ship"

MAUREEN O'HARA   Introduction Of Second Act
PRINCESS THEATRE WORKSHOP
Scene · "World Series";   Actors John Bates & Yvonne Griffin

PAT BOONE   Introduction of Pianist
Don Morris
Plays: Chopin's   "Sonata Presto"

MAUREEN O'HARA and PAT BOONE   Introduction to Third Act
STANFORD UNIVERSITY
Scene · "Terma"; Actors · Gene Parseghian & Mary Staton

**The first speaker at the American Theatre
Awards was Joe Houser, vice president of the
California-Hawaii Elks Association.**

VARIETY

LEGIT REVIEW

MARY STATON AND ERIC SERVER WIN AMERICAN THEATRE AWARDS

Accent of the first annual American Theatre Awards pageant was on young thesps in development being given exposure to high-powered studio and theatrical exec. This was accomplished at Santa Monica Civic Auditorium Monday night, even though (like many award ceremonies) production may have overextended itself. It became a little gruelling before its three hours were up.

By the time trophies to Mr. and Miss California Theatre Awards and to competing acting schools were presented, little suspense was left, and attention was focused on winners' tears of joy.

Eric Server, a theatre-arts major at Santa Monica City College, and Mary Staton, graduate drama student at Stanford, copped best actor and actress awards and won berths in the future national playoffs.

Server was the only double winner of the 10 competing thesps as SMCC's entry, a scene from an original play, "The Miracle and the Boar," in which Cathy Warren also appeared, took first place in the school competition.

The Monday affair was playoff of competition started last Jan. 25 when Benevolent and Protective Order of Elks established the program for theatrical schools and workshops. Finalists were selected from 18 entries that vied in the same auditorium in January.

BPOE's object is to establish award competish nation-wide, although first event was limited to California. Produced by J. Herbert Klein, pageant was an impressive initial effort with format loosely following Oscar award ceremonies.

Emceed by Pat Boone and Maureen O'Hara, program alternated competing scenes with variety acts, including comedian Lou Alexander, SMCC all-girl drill team, and participants eligible for the Mario Lanza Memorial Award.

Latter is a new award being set up by the late singer's mother, Mary Lanza, to be integrated into the BPOE program. Entertainers included singers Mark Richardson, Dorothy Harpell and Arthur Ross Jones, pianist Don Morris, and violinist Endre Balogh.

Competition was judged by Robert Wise, producers Jack Cummings and Sol Baer Fielding, James A. Doolittle, fan-mag writer May Mann, comedienne Patti Moore, Dr. Julius White of USC drama department, and talent scouts Al Trescony (MGM), Jack Roberts (W7), and Curt Conway, (20th-Fox).

Panel rated entrants by place, tapping SMCC first, UCLA second, Estelle Harmon Workshop third, Stanford fourth, and Princess Theatre Workshop fifth.

UCLA was repped by Judy Kaye (currently appearing as Lucy in Irv's "You're A Good Man, Charlie Brown") and Robert Carricart Jr., in a scene from Anouilh's "The Lark."

Richard Sweeney and Barbara

Mallory presented their original comedy scene, "The First Night," as the Estelle Harmon entry.

Miss Staton's award was based on her performance as "Yerma," Stanford's entry, in which Gene Parseghian also appeared. Princess thesps John Batis and Yvonne Griffin acted a scene from an original, "The World Series," by Paul Schneider.

Each group was presented a trophy, in ascending order, by Julie Parrish, James MacArthur, Yvonne Craig, Yale Summers and Marilyn Maxwell.

Some 1,800 attended the event, which, according to program notes, gives "the aspiring young actor ... valuable exposure, plus the opportunity to advance in his chosen profession. At the same time, a fresh source of exciting new talent is made available to motion pictures, television and the stage."

David Tihmar directed the gala which, as a kick-off effort, was quite remarkable, auguring another annual awards event likely to achieve major importance.

Daily Variety called the American Theatre Awards, "...quite remarkable, auguring another annual awards event likely to achieve major importance."

The lovely and talented Maureen O'Hara – one of the biggest stars of all time – was co-host of the American Theatre Awards, the Elks-sponsored talent competition I produced during the 1960s.

I'd love to continue the tradition of the American Theatre Awards with a program called *Stars of Tomorrow*. This time, we'd focus on high schools – with each lodge sponsoring at least one high school in its area. Each state's winner would compete regionally, and the finalists would come to Hollywood for a televised gala event and selection of the grand-prize winners.

For the competitions, the high school's cinema arts and dramatic arts departments would prepare short programs that would be judged on overall production values, acting and directing, cinematography, writing, and other categories – think the Oscars on a smaller scale.

I feel that *Stars of Tomorrow* could be just what the Elks needs to attract younger members and get the students and their parents excited about the organization and appreciate its abundant benefits. If the Elks are willing, I'm ready and able to help!

AFTERWORD

When I joined the Elks in 1951, I was a young husband, father, business owner, builder, as well as a movie producer. And those were the days before cell phones, computers, and the Internet. It's hard to fathom sometimes how we managed to get everything done – but we always found time to spend at our Elks lodge.

The Elks, for me, was a way to connect with my fellows, to socialize, to feel part of something bigger than myself, to give back to the community, and make the world a better place. Those are still the reasons I cherish my membership in the Elks.

The Elks are truly the Best People On Earth, and I wrote this book in gratitude for an Order that has done so much for humanity, for the world, and has made me proud to call myself a member.

BIBLIOGRAPHY

Detweiler, Meade D. *An Account of the Origin and Early History of the Benevolent and Protective Order of the Elks of the U.S.A.* Harrisburg, PA: Harrisburg Publishing Company, 1898.

Ellis, Charles Edward. *The Authentic History of the Benevolent and Protective Order of Elks.* Chicago: Charles Edward Ellis Publications, 1910.

Nicholson, James R. *History of the Order of Elks (1868-1952),* New York: National Memorial and Publication Commission of the Benevolent and Protective Order of Elks of the United States of America, 1953.

Rituals of Special Services Benevolent and Protective Order of Elks of the United States of America, 1925.

The Elks National Memorial. The Grand Lodge of the Benevolent and Protective Order of Elks of the United States of America, published under the supervision of the Elks National Memorial and Publication Commission, 1931.

What It Means to Be an Elk. Chicago, IL: Benevolent and Protective Order of Elks.

AUTHOR BIOGRAPHY

J. HERBERT KLEIN was born in Detroit, Michigan, on August 22, 1921. He joined the U.S. Army Air Corps in 1942 and served in the First Motion Picture Unit, where Captain Ronald W. Reagan was his superior officer. After his release from the service in 1945, Klein took over the family business – building luxury homes for the rich and famous. In 1956, Klein and colleague Charles Martin produced the film noir classic *Death of a Scoundrel*, the last movie that Howard Hughes financed. Subsequently, Klein pioneered talk television, producing programs that appeared on local stations in Los Angeles. In 1968, Klein produced the first American Theatre Awards, a talent competition for college students judged by Hollywood legends such as Robert Wise, director of *West Side Story* and *The Sound of Music*. During the mid-1960s, Klein established a business partnership with Jon Hall, leading man of the 1930s and 1940s, that generated patents and technological innovations. One of the oldest members of the Academy of Motion Picture Arts and Sciences and the Academy of Television Arts and Sciences, Klein is still active in the business as executive producer of International Film Arts – a production company that develops projects for film and television. Klein has been a B.P.O.E. member since 1951.

CPSIA information can be obtained at www.ICGtesting.com
Printed in the USA
LVOW012148170112

264360LV00007B/169/P

9 780983 028079